INTERNATIONAL PROJECT MANAGEMENT

OWEN JAY MURPHY,
M.B.A., BSEE

Australia · Canada · Mexico · Singapore · Spain · United Kingdom · United States

INTERNATIONAL PROJECT MANAGEMENT
Owen Jay Murphy, M.B.A., BSEE

Library of Congress Cataloging in Publication Number is available. See page 224 for details.

For more information about our products, contact us at:

Thomson Learning Academic Resource Center
1-800-423-0563

Thomson Higher Education
5191 Natorp Boulevard
Mason, Ohio 45040
USA

Asia (including India)
Thomson Learning
5 Shenton Way
#01-01 UIC Building
Singapore 068808

Australia/New Zealand
Thomson Learning Australia
102 Dodds Street
Southbank, Victoria 3006
Australia

Canada
Thomson Nelson
1120 Birchmount Road
Toronto, Ontario
M1K 5G4
Canada

Latin America
Thomson Learning
Seneca, 53
Colonia Polanco
11560 Mexico
D.F. Mexico

UK/Europe/Middle East/Africa
Thomson Learning
High Holborn House
50/51 Bedford Row
London WC1R 4LR
United Kingdom

Spain (including Portugal)
Thomson Paraninfo
Calle Magallanes, 25
28015 Madrid, Spain

TABLE OF CONTENTS

ACKNOWLEDGEMENTS

The transition from writing technical reports, white papers, and management summaries to publication in business journals and writing a book on international business was arduous. Writing classes at the state university and association with other aspiring writers were helpful.

Though during the many hours and days while I was working on this book, there was no one sitting beside me at my desk, pen in hand, or at the keyboard to share in the selection of contents, choice of words, or construction of sentences, to claim that this work was mine alone would not be honest. A number of people contributed to the final product.

Phil Reed, author of *Birddog* and *Low Rider*, was one instructor whom I credit with inspiring me to pick up a pen and start the actual first step. The encouragement of my association of aspiring writers, including Ed Pallette, M.D, Larry Porricelli, Ofra Obejas, and Pam Rocke was instrumental in helping to keep me on track. Their honest appraisals of my efforts were greatly appreciated.

But this book is not about writing. This book is about managing international projects. Though I have credentials for writing on this topic, the world is too big and varied for the experience of any one person to cover everything, so I called upon the expertise of others to augment my own. The most valuable experience I drew upon was that of a friend and former boss, Vernon Platt. A former vice president of Hughes Aircraft Company's Ground Systems Group, Vernon spent more than 30 years working in the international arena. I am indebted to him for his careful review of the drafts of the manuscript and his pointed, often critical, comments. We have been friends for many years, have traveled overseas together both for business and with our wives for vacations, and enjoy our annual motorcycle rides across the Western United States. I respect his opinion on matters of international business.

I would also like to thank the staff of Thomson/South-Western for recognizing the potential of this book, and for the several offers of encouragement and patience. Michael Jeffers and Steve Momper of the editorial staff were particularly helpful in the early stages of the writing. Barbara Evans' assistance in the production and composition of the book was invaluable, and Cathy Coleman of the marketing department provided excellent guidance for the marketing of the book as well as personal encouragement during a particularly trying period. There were a number of other involved in the development of the book whose names I don't know, and I thank each of them.

Credit also goes to my late wife and family, partly for putting up with a grouchy old man wrestling with difficult points, but mostly for their encouragement. Anita is the one who said, "You can do it." Most important, she would not have said so if she hadn't meant it.

To all these, I owe my deepest gratitude. Though I haven't always thanked them at the time for the support, I do so here.

ABOUT THE AUTHOR

Owen Jay Murphy is a writer, communications engineer, and international marketer who has managed a large number of international projects. He spent over 20 years working in international business, and learned the ins and outs first hand. He has earned both a B.S. in electronics engineering and an M.B.A.

In his many years of corporate experience in the aerospace industry, Mr. Murphy served as a communications engineer, marketing manager, and project manager in Greece, Germany, Italy, Portugal, France, Denmark, United Kingdom, Egypt, Jordan, Saudi Arabia, Pakistan, Korea, Japan, Singapore, Thailand, Taiwan, and Malaysia. Each of these countries and each of these experiences enriched his knowledge of the international marketplace and of the difficulties arising from differences in customs, language, cultures, and business practices. He has many successes to his credit, but he has also suffered at times when he failed to heed his own advice. He learned from that.

Mr. Murphy contributes regularly to a local business journal on a variety of business and community subjects, as well as editing the writings of others for the same journal.

Mr. Murphy lives in Southern California, where he is active in his community as a member of the board of several community organizations, serving on such committees as publications, information services, investment, and fund development. He is an officer in the local chapter of the Military Officers Association of America, works with adult literacy projects, and is active with the Chamber of Commerce.

CHAPTER 1
GOING INTERNATIONAL

The thought of managing an international project conjures visions of exotic locations, foods, and people; first-class hotels and five-star restaurants; not to mention strange customs, unknown environments, and potential risks. There is also the prestige that goes with this responsibility and the potential of another step up the company promotion ladder. The newly assigned manager experiences pride and anticipation mixed with anxiety.

This emotional mixture is well founded. The pride, because not every project manager will be selected to lead an international project. The anticipation, because the exciting places and people he will meet with in the global arena along with the probable positive career move, is certainly exhilarating. But the anxiety is justified as well. It is a fact of business life that many international projects fail—projects that have been underestimated, poorly planned, or poorly managed; projects in which the customer and contractor had significantly different views of what was to be accomplished; and projects that simply buckled under too many unplanned and unforeseen events. That is why an international project can make or break a project manager's career. Following the guidelines in this book should greatly improve his or her chances of success.

In addition to the challenges every domestic project manager faces, the international project manager faces unique situations. Foreign hotel accommodations clearly overpriced at $3 a night and much of the restaurant fare is cause for the project manager to long for the canned stew of Boy Scout days. More broadly, each continent, each country, has its own culture and its own set of business customs and laws that will not be modified to accommodate any American company. Whether the project is a simple import-export operation, the building of a toll road in an undeveloped country, the expansion of the telecommunications infrastructure, or a multimillion-dollar defense contract, the project manager is in for fascinating experiences, exciting challenges, and unforeseen risks that can easily undermine the success of the project.

In more than 20 years of managing international projects, I never found a definitive guide to help me perform my responsibilities to make a project succeed to the expectations of the company. All I had to go on were the anecdotal lessons of those who had gone before. Like all anecdotes, their lessons were slanted toward the view of the person telling the story. Still, adding those lessons to my own experiences, both good and bad, I acquired a wealth of knowledge about managing international projects.

Over the years I gained a healthy respect for the use of financial controls to help manage projects. Their effective use can expose weak points in project planning; they can help the manager anticipate and be prepared to respond to delays and technical problems and find alternate ways to meet milestones and goals.

Using the tools requires discipline on the part of all project team members. In this book, the controls, are referred to as *management tools, project control tools,* and *financial control tools,* depending on the context. The terms are interchangeable.

On international commercial projects, the use of financial controls is at the discretion of the contractor, who should exercise the option. On international projects that have an American customer, such as foreign military sales (FMS) projects with some element of the U.S. government as the program executive (customer, in our terminology), the controls will be imposed on the contractor. (In these cases the *ultimate* customer, the foreign government, is referred to as the *end user*.)

I also learned the value of a rigorous risk-management system. Risks are almost always, by definition, difficult to quantify; probabilities of the occurrence of specific events are even more difficult calculate with any accuracy. This difficulty of quantification often leads managers to have less confidence in the system. As a result, most risk management efforts fail early in the project. But you ignore risks at peril of your project. I include in this book a methodology for managing risks that has proved both accurate and successful over many years and many projects.

This book is both a guidebook and a reference manual for those managing projects outside the United States. However, managers of domestic as well as international projects will find the book useful because most project tasks are the same for both. In any case, for projects destined for other countries, much of the effort is performed in-plant in the United States, especially when there is significant new development. Done properly, the in-plant phase will eliminate many of the risks of the overseas phase as well as making it easier.

The book clearly explains how to deal with the challenges the manager will face overseas. You will learn how to anticipate and recognize many of the situations that will arise throughout the life of a project. What you learn will be of invaluable help in dealing with customs, risks, and opportunities in the international market, and you will build the skills you need to deal with these situations as they arise. Specifically, you will learn:

- *Considerations to be taken into account in pursuing projects and business overseas.* The two main reasons are higher profit potential and the company growth that can result from increased international business. You will also be made aware of the risks and how to eliminate or mitigate them. For nonprofit operations, considerations relate not to profit but to success measured in different terms, such as completion of the project within budget and time constraints, and satisfaction of the social or political need that spawned the project in the first place.

- *How to tap into available resources, both* government and private, to find contacts worldwide, and how to turn a contact into a customer.

- *How to deal with the cultures likely to be encountered* in the social as well as business environment. The two environments tend to be tightly bound in international business cultures because business is often conducted during social events, such as dinners.

- *How to organize project staff and tasks,* taking into consideration the cultural environment, management tools available, special skills required, and possible customer participation. The course set in the early stages has extreme leverage on the results of the project, for good or ill.

- *How to use financial controls* to manage the project to a successful and profitable conclusion. A good project plan uses effective financial controls to assure that milestones are met and project success is achieved.

- *How to identify and manage the risks* associated with the project. You will learn to evaluate each risk in terms of dollars, estimate the probability and likely timing of a risk occurring, and monitor each risk all the way to elimination or closure.

- *How to manage in-country activities* including housing and transportation, incentives, administration, and supervision.

- *How to control final evaluation and customer acceptance (sell-off)* of the project. International projects must be managed up to the last minute of the last day, or the profit potential will disappear quickly. Every phase is important. Although it can happen in any project, the potential for costs increasing rapidly at the end of the project are greater overseas than at home. The reasons are covered in the last section of the book.

The points presented in this book will be demonstrated in terms of a sample project: to build a log cabin of American design and primarily American materials, incorporating major systems and subsystems, in an imaginary foreign country called Europistania. For each system and subsystem there must be tradeoff studies, analysis, risk assessment, and integration into the master plan and master schedule. The major systems are:

- Land preparation.
- Structure system.
- Access system.
- Power system.
- Plumbing system.
- Heating and air conditioning system.
- Communications system.

I chose this project because I know almost nothing about building a log cabin. It allows me to concentrate on the *process of project management in an international environment* and not on the nature of the work itself. And because Europistania is a figment of my imagination, its customs, laws, and practices are not specific to any region of the world.

In this book, the terms *international, overseas,* and *foreign* are used interchangeably. In this context, Mexico is overseas but Hawaii is not. Also, though I have tried to avoid the use of trite in-vogue buzzwords that are intended to convey more insight and meaning than might actually exist, in at least two cases I am obliged to use the terminology unique to the discipline. These exceptions are the quality system and the financial control system. Even with those exceptions, this book is written to be easy to read and understand so that the busy manager can use his valuable time on the actual work.

In this book, I provide the tools necessary to enable a reader to plan, staff, organize, and manage the project effectively; to foresee and plan for the inevitable risks; and to recover from unforeseen events along the path to success.

It is important for any project that its manager start off on the right foot. It is even more important in international projects where the risks are more severe, the costs higher, and the innate difficulty of recovering from negative events. There are numerous examples of projects that were doomed from the start, projects no amount of effort, no matter how valiant, could turn around. As I will reiterate throughout the book, these failures usually result from poor planning early in the project. Here are typical examples:

> Negotiations were stalled because the customer was insisting on some unfavorable terms. Though the two sides were making progress, slowly, execution of the contract would clearly be delayed into the following fiscal year, a situation unpleasant to upper management. A senior manager stated that he could get the customer to agree in time to book the sale in the current fiscal period. However, when he traveled to the customer's offices, he simply agreed to the unfavorable terms. The project manager was left to clean up the mess later—which turned out to be impossible. This was a clear example of the old adage, if the project is priced low enough, any marketer can sell it.
>
> During the negotiation and planning phases, the manager assigned to the project went on vacation. A replacement manager was sent to continue the effort and, not being familiar with all the details, agreed to terms accepting a suite of customer-provided equipment. Because that equipment proved inadequate for the job, the company lost significant money on the project.

The goal of our business endeavors is to make a profit. For the project manager, that translates into the need to control costs to keep within budget. Even a nonprofit organization must remain within budget, and the difference between budgeted and final costs can be thought of as the profit or loss on the project, which is an indication of its success. The business must thrive in order to improve the wealth of the owners, pay the salaries of employees, and contribute to the well-being of the community. Making a profit is an honorable and necessary goal for private business, but unforeseen risks place the success of the project, and possibly the firm, in jeopardy.

Some organizations, however, exist primarily to provide a service to their customers. Decisions made by managers are intended not to maximize profits but to maximize service within the constraints of available resources. Nonprofit organizations are measured by how much of what they offer they actually provide to their customers, but that too depends on how well they stay within budget allocations.

The guidance provided in this book applies to nonprofit as well as for-profit organizations. Project managers in either case have a budget they are required to manage so that they can complete their tasks. If the project manager complies with the budgetary and time constraints, the parent organization will make its profit or meet its service goals. There is little difference between the jobs of the two project managers.

As I have already said several times, the early phases of the project are critical to its success. The manager must thoroughly understand and accept the details of the program as spelled out in the contract. For a program to be successful and profitable—and it must be profitable to be successful—it has to be completed on time, to the satisfaction of the customer. That means every element of the work statement must be completed as and when agreed. Schedule delays—slips, set-overs, whatever they may be called—are fatal to profits on a fixed price contract.

Every manager I know, including myself, has been told by senior managers that:

- Every manager should anticipate all risks ahead of time.

- Projects require different leaders in each phase (contract planning, execution, test, closeout).

- Increases in corporate assessed costs can be absorbed by the project with no loss of profit.

- Errors of previous phases can be made up in future phases of the project.
- Any good manager can manage any project.

Experienced managers know that not one of these statements is true. Managers do not have an innate talent for anticipating risks; they need a systematic way to identify and manage the risks. When corporate management assesses additional costs beyond those in the plans, the profit potential—if not the planned profit—decreases. Errors are usually compounded rather than made up; and not every manager is right for every project.

The manager's abilities in all the aspects of project management make the difference between success and failure on any project. Managing an international project taxes those abilities to a degree not experienced in domestic projects. They will tax not only the manager's skills but also those of his technical and functional staffs, not to mention the support the corporation gives to the project in terms of standardized processes, trained personnel, and efficient. (In this context, the word *standard* refers to processes and tasks that have written procedures mandated by the company.)

Standard processes, though necessary, will not by themselves guarantee success. Our experience with the ISO 9000 series of certifications and with various quality management systems developed through the years, from Zero Defects to Six Sigma, has proven the value of standard processes. At the very least, they force the company to plan and document a process and then adhere to the plan. By continually improving the process, making it more efficient and reliable, they ensure both efficient work and a good product, which will result in on-time delivery to a satisfied customer.

The weakness in the theory is that good processes do not automatically result in a good project. This is a fatal flaw for those who believe that any "system" will solve project problems. Systems are tools to be used by skillful managers, not solutions to problems in and of themselves. Only those processes that have brought about on-time performance of the projects they support can benefit the company.

To be effective, the processes have to be in place in time to train the staff to use them. They must have been practiced and proven before the project starts. Otherwise, they may turn out to be tailored for a specific project and of little use on others.

During negotiations with the customer as well as during project planning, the processes that will be used have to be well defined. Otherwise, the project manager may be surprised by the costs and time requirements of using standard processes.

One huge quirk in the delivery of a project to a customer is that there is *one* product item to one customer. A single example is not a good candidate for statistical analysis. Customer satisfaction is measured not by reduced errors per million but by how well the contractual delivery requirements are met. The project manager must focus on this project for *this* customer.

Managing an international project does expand the manager's capabilities. It broadens and stretches the manager's imagination and ability to apply it to more issues, more nuances, greater risks, and greater difficulties, as well as to exploit greater opportunities. In thus broadening the manager's experience, it increases his worth to the company.

So gather up your day planner or PDA and get ready for an interesting journey.

PART I
GETTING STARTED

CHAPTER 2
THE CONTEXT OF
INTERNATIONAL PROJECTS

There are compelling reasons to take your business international, but before doing so, management must consider the risks and downsides as well as the opportunities in the global arena. All business endeavors contain elements of both risk and opportunity. When the opportunities outweigh the risks, the business has a chance of winning. The difference with the international arena is that without thorough preparation and knowledge of the environment, the risks are higher, and opportunities may be easily missed.

There are global markets for all types of American products, services, and technology. Consumer goods are highly desired in spite of the higher prices they often command. U.S. technology, the best in the world today, is sought after by many overseas governments and businesses. American companies can compete favorably for such international projects as constructing roads, building factories, and improving national infrastructure systems for power, fuel distribution, and communications.

There is also a military market in much of the world that is open to American businesses. This is a specialized area of business that requires comprehensive knowledge of the defense industry. Many of the large and small businesses that have some experience with government contracts, either as a prime or a subcontractor, are in a position to seek business in the military market. Others can gain that knowledge, but this is a particularly risky area.

REASONS TO PURSUE INTERNATIONAL BUSINESS

Reasons for moving into the international arena vary greatly from business to business, from person to person, but main ones are the potential for larger profits and the resulting company growth. In spite of the many issues that have to be addressed when a company decides to go international, the potential for increased profits is too significant to ignore. The profits from overseas operations keep many companies afloat in otherwise unfavorable economic times at home, allowing them to weather the domestic storm and survive as an economic entity.

> Some companies get into international business almost by accident. One company in Southern California accepted a contract to build a lamination plant in Germany after a former machinery supplier approached them. Though the builder was inexperienced in international business and projects, the customer provided all the necessary support except the U.S. export licenses to make the project successful. From that project, the company acquired the credentials it needed to expand into other countries.

Some companies get requests for proposals from all over the world through their Internet Web sites.

However the business gets started, the goals are the same—to expand the business and to improve the profits.

Almost any overseas region can offer an expanded market for a company's products or services. The more developed and wealthier countries are the first to come to mind and certainly offer a lucrative market, but even those that are not yet industrialized can be profitable for American products. They may even offer a better opportunity. As those countries develop their industrial base, there will be more business for those who have already established business relationships there.

The story is told in M.B.A. marketing classes of two shoe salesmen who went to Southeast Asia some years ago to find a market for their product. The first sent a communication to the home office that there was no market in that country because the citizens didn't wear shoes. The second communicated to the home office that the market was huge since at present no one owned any shoes.

By expanding overseas, a company can also extend the life cycle of its products beyond that normally expected in a purely domestic environment. Extending the life cycle places the product in the mature, "cash cow," phase of the product life cycle because the costs of development and the product's "infant mortality" warranties have already been absorbed, which greatly improves the margins.

There are synergies between domestic and international markets. Most companies experience a resurgence of domestic sales as a direct or indirect result of increased overseas sales. The resulting increase in sales serves to improve overall market share of the products. Partly, the improvement is due to the continued marketing campaign to support the international sales and partly to the global nature of our economy today.

In the defense market, developmental military items will not normally be readily available for international sales. Only after the U.S. military has completed its purchase program will it consider requests for foreign sales. Approvals for such requests are often delayed for years, so while there is synergy between domestic and international military sales, there is a significant time lag.

Going international tends to smooth out the business cycles experienced in the United States. Certainly, all other economies experience economic cycles, both as a nature of business and as a result, again, of the global nature of world economies. However, the cycles of other countries are rarely in synch with that of the United States, giving international businesses the opportunity to benefit from the favorable portion of the cycle in other parts of the world during the down phase at home. This is much like diversifying your personal stock portfolio.

Many businesses, especially those in the manufacturing sector, depend on large labor forces and the prices of their products reflect these costs. For many years now, we've seen much of the labor-intensive manufacturing sector move overseas to locations with more favorable wage rates. As wage rates in those countries rise, the migration continues as other countries become prime locations. Note, however, that there are financial and social as well as political costs involved in moving manufacturing out of this country, and those costs have to be compared to the benefits derived from the move.

Some countries (like most U.S. states) offer benefits, such as government-sponsored capital investment or a tax-free period to encourage businesses to relocate to their area. These incentives offer long-term stability for companies choosing to make the move, and there are few things that benefit businesses more than economic stability.

In sum, there are essentially four reasons to take your business into the international arena:

1. Increase profits.
2. Grow the company.
3. Smooth out business cycles.
4. Extend the sales potential of existing products.

All require work and all require careful planning. There are also downsides as well as risks to be considered.

CULTURAL ISSUES

One of the first questions I'm asked when addressing the international marketplace inevitably has to do with cultural issues, such as language, customs, or laws. The concept of culture is so complex that even anthropologists have difficulty agreeing on a single definition. It can be considered the distinctive way of life of a people of a geographic region or specific ethnicity. It includes their views on material objects as well as their language, types and styles of art, education systems, religion and belief systems, social interactions and organizations, and political life and structures. Social scientists can probably cite many more attributes. I will look only at those aspects of culture that impact business practices.

Cultural issues that impact business practices take many forms. There are local customs that guide the behavior in a country, or even regions of a country. For example, the state of Bavaria in Germany has some customs that are unique and that differ from those of the rest of Germany. Even the daily greeting is different.

Social amenities differ among countries. Most important to business-people trying to expand operations into the international market, there are customary business practices that can differ significantly from those of the United States.

RACIAL ISSUES

I'm often asked about racial discrimination in the international markets, but in over 20 years of work overseas, I've only encountered one instance. The company I supported was asked by its Saudi customer to exclude from the proposed project employees of Jewish ethnicity and religion as well as any-one from the Palestinian Territories, whether they were citizens of the United States or another country.

Local customs are usually recognized as such by the local business-people with whom you'll interface. Except as a topic of dinner conversation, those customs will have little impact on your day-to-day activities. There are exceptions, however.

WEEKENDS IN THE MIDDLE EAST

A typical local custom that will impact your business operations is that the weekend in many Islamic countries is on Thursday and Friday. Since few offices in the United States are open on Saturday and Sunday, that leaves only Monday, Tuesday and Wednesday available for communications between U.S. offices and those of the customer. When you set up operations in those countries, you will be expected to abide by this type of local custom. With today's ubiquitous Internet access, earlier inconveniences have largely been eliminated except for the overseas staff, which now finds itself working almost every day of the week.

BUSINESS/SOCIAL EVENTS AND WOMEN

In many Asian and Middle-Eastern countries, where much of the business is conducted during after-hours socializing and the societies are male-dominated, female managers will find it awkward, if not impossible, to partici-pate in the social activities. I know of many Asian businesses owned by women but with the husband or eldest son as the representative to the public. I'm familiar with a business in Saudi Arabia that is owned by a woman but hardly anyone doing business with her company has met her. Her eldest son is the face of the business. Though it's no secret where the power lies in that company, it's not a subject of formal discussion. This may seem unfair to those of us who are accustomed to more equal roles for men and women, but if you want to do business in another country, it's not wise to take on the additional burden of transforming the customs of that country. It's not good for business.

In many cases, and for diverse reasons, it's not practical to replace your female manager with a male stand-in. She will have to be the one who faces the customer even during social engagements. Many female managers have been successful in these environs. Here are a few thoughts that can help the female executive or project manager have successful interactions:

- Particularly in Asia, remember that your peers are the men, not the women present. Keep this in mind at all times. Be polite to the women, but remember that you are there for business, not part of the entertainment.

- Dress attractively, but not seductively. It's not necessary to wear a suit, though that's always appropriate, and all you are looking for is business-appropriate attire. Should you choose to wear a dress, it should be cosmopolitan, tasteful, and relatively conservative — meaning arms and shoulders covered and no low cleavage. Skirt length should extend below the knee. Nylons should be worn and are in fact always appropriate. Open-toed shoes and sandals are never appropriate.

- Check local customs for color. Wearing the color black in Italy is not appropriate unless it is accented with lots of color, because it represents death and mourning. Red is not appropriate in most Asian environments, and yellow is a color reserved for royalty in Thailand and some other areas, so avoid those colors in those locales.

- Do not overindulge in alcohol, though the males may appear to. There are tricks the experienced Asian businessmen use to avoid too much alcohol in spite of how much they seem to drink. The person most sober at the end of the evening wins. Women have the advantage over men in this area since they can refuse a drink without criticism. In fact, due to the potential embarrassment of the host should a female "win," it would be better not to participate.

- Jokes do not translate well. Most topics are acceptable for social conversation, but you will find that jokes don't translate well between languages and cultures. Unless you are certain that your favorite one has universal appeal, resist the temptation.

- In discussing family and children, keep it short, and avoid personal details. Women in business should not discuss their children unless asked. If you are asked about them, answer the questions and guide the discussion back to the business at hand. I have witnessed too many occasions of someone carrying the discourse far too long once given the opening. And it's not always the women in the group.

- Be able to discuss international politics, but avoid confrontation. U.S. international policy is a favorite subject throughout the world, and the tone of the discussion is generally negative. Be aware of how local businessmen and politicians feel about U.S. politics, and be able to discuss the issues intelligently but without confrontation. Americans are considered by much of the rest of the world to be naive and blindly pro-American—though, in fact, that can be said of the citizens of most countries. To be able to discuss the issues from your host's point of view, even while disagreeing with him, earns his respect.

- Be prepared to have to sit on the floor at restaurants in many Asian countries. Wearing pants is a perfect solution, but if you wear a dress or skirt, make sure it is long enough and loose enough to enable you to remain covered while so seated. Avoid shoes with overly high heels.

- Keep jewelry simple. Bracelets should not be ostentatious, nor should they jingle. Earrings should be small and simple. Jewelry can be expensive or not, but never showy.

- Women's hair should be treated differently for business and personal activities. Hair, like jewelry, should not be flashy in a business environment. Long hair requires special attention to avoid attracting too much attention away from the matters at hand.

- Do not dress too casually even on your day off sightseeing. Leave the shorts at home. Blue jeans are not appropriate for either men or women. Slacks, shirt or blouse, and blazer are considered casual dress in most of the world. You won't be allowed in most religious buildings in shorts or sandals, and you'll need something to cover your head, such as a scarf, in most churches, synagogues, mosques, and other religious environs.

- Buy a guidebook for the area you're visiting to ascertain the local dress customs, and buy a book on business dress. In these days of casual business dress, it is often difficult to know the rules. If you take a look at most CEOs today, you will observe that even the female executives wear a suit. Take their lead.

Social issues can be handled with normal good manners and concern for the other person. The interested manager can quickly learn the cultural differences. The higher the position of the manager, the more attention will be given to her social skills. A social klutz at a high level can do untold, often irreparable, damage to a business relationship.

An example of a social klutz that I witnessed complained to all those nearby that the host was rude and failed to compliment his wife upon their arrival at the restaurant. He didn't realize that in that country, it is considered impolite to show interest in another man's wife. In any case, the businessmen of that country don't bring their wives to business-related parties. They bring women that indicate their power and wealth.

Some other examples of the more common faux pas that have embarrassed the hosts of American businessmen are:

- Asking for a T-bone steak in a German Gasthaus, which serves only traditional cuisine of the country. Butchers in other countries don't cut the meat as do ours.

- Failing to understand that a martini in Europe is just the vermouth sans gin or vodka.

- Making fun of the driving habits of typical European, whose driving customs and rules differ from our own.

Obviously, it's not just the T-bone steak, the martini, or the driving habits that are the issues. Many things that are customary to us are unknown or different elsewhere. The astute traveler needs to be alert to the fact that these matters will surface, and be able to address them with care and courtesy.

There are literally hundreds, maybe thousands, of differences between our customs and those of other countries. The successful businessperson in an international environment welcomes these differences, studies them, and becomes skilled in dealing with unusual circumstances.

AGE MATTERS

Particularly in Asia, but also in many European, African, and South American cultures, age is important. Your counterpart will be very close to your own age, and asking of your age is considered an appropriate question, no different from asking your position in your company. You will socialize with those close to your own age, and business is often conducted during social activities. The implication is that to deal with upper management, your own representative will have to be of about the same age (within five years for those over 35, less for those younger). In these cultures, little value is assigned to those who have risen to high levels at a young age. They believe our culture, which allows such advancement, is less sophisticated than their own. You are operating in their environment, and their rules apply.

FORMALITY PREVAILS

The American tendency to call everyone by their first names is too casual for most businesspeople outside the United States. Until you are invited to do otherwise, use Mr., Mrs., or Miss or the military rank, as appropriate. Ms. is also appropriate, but the person so referred will usually advise you of her marital status. If she does, use the appropriate title.

There is a protocol to offering a business card that American business-people often ignore both in this country and overseas. The proper way to offer a card is face up with the card facing so that the receiver can read it. The card should be offered with both hands. In many countries it's considered impolite to offer anything with one hand. When receiving a card, take it with both hands and study it. Treat it with dignity. Either leave it on the table in front of you (at a meeting) or put it away carefully, as though it had value. Never write on it. If you have to make notes, do so on another piece of paper, not on the card. The American habit of reaching into a coat pocket and "flicking" a card out between the index finger and forefinger, offering it to someone without even looking at it, is considered not only impolite, but rude even in America.

The form of communication in international matters is important. Phone conversations, faxes, and e-mails are considered informal. They will not meet the requirements for formal notification of contractual, or contractually important, matters. Any communication that you wish to become formal has to be followed up with a letter referencing the prior, informal, communication. Even the letter must be on company letterhead, signed by a person recognized in the contract as so authorized. Many a company has made the error of thinking it had notified the customer of an event only to find that the receiver didn't accept the notice as "formal," resulting in an unintentional violation of the contract—and, most likely, delayed payments.

LANGUAGE ISSUES

Certainly, English has become the language of business, even the language of diplomacy. English is ubiquitous as a second language throughout the world. It is very common to sit in the lounge of a hotel in Seoul or Tokyo and listen to two or more Asian businesspeople discussing matters in English. The same is largely true in Europe.

English words have more precise definitions than we Americans normally assign them, but those who have studied English as a foreign language understand that precision. If you are careless with your selection of words, you may have problems, because your customer will be reading your communications with more thought and care than you used in the writing, and that can cause both embarrassment on your part and, worse, misunderstanding on his.

Precise selection of words and phrases is important. Prepare your written communications so that they cannot be misunderstood or misinterpreted, using simple declarative sentences and careful selection of words. Avoid compound sentences. Compound sentences that express more than a single thought will be misunderstood. Your customer does not hesitate to use a dictionary. You should use one, too.

Napoleon had a corporal read his orders before he issued them to his officers. He reasoned that if the uneducated corporal could understand them, the officers would not misinterpret them.

It is of little hindrance to business transactions to speak only English and to have the contract prepared in English. In fact, this is common, the norm, and it's rare to be in a locale that isn't comfortable with these terms.

Often contracts will be prepared in both English and the language of the host country. This makes sense, because there will be some members of the customer's organization who are not fluent in English but who need to understand the contract. However, having two versions of the contract can cause difficulties.

> In one case with which I'm familiar, it was agreed that the Arabic language version of the contract was the one that would be in force. The two parties then proceeded to alter the terms of the contract using the English language version. After several weeks and more travel back and forth, negotiations were completed and both parties signed the Arabic version, which had not been altered. It was not until the project was in the test and evaluation phase that the contractor learned of his error. He was forced to honor the Arabic version of the contract at his own cost.

FOODS OF ALL VARIETIES

Next to language, foods distinguish the various cultures of the world. Many of the favorite foods of a country are strange to Americans. For instance, Scotland has its haggis; Germany, its blood sausage; Vietnam has Snake Alley (appropriately named); Japan, its sushi and sashimi; and Norway, its raw herring breakfast. England even has local cuisine, though it is difficult to find without local help.

Many American foods, on the other hand, are not especially tasty to foreign guests. For instance, the American pizza is not well liked by Italians who prefer not to mix foods. A four-ingredient pizza in Italy will have four quadrants of one ingredient each. In fact, with the exception of the Chinese, who tend to prefer to eat in Chinese restaurants even in America, our Americanized versions of international dishes are not well received by international guests.

Always ask what kind of food your guests would like to try. Normally, they will ask for "a typical American restaurant." In this case, a steakhouse is the best bet. That's the best-known American-style restaurant.

As an exception to the rule, I had a general from the Italian Army request an Italian restaurant. I chose a restaurant whose owners were from Italy. I asked that they serve Italian-style, which includes several courses of small servings, instead of the single larger servings normally preferred by Americans, and that the waiters speak Italian. The owner's sons acted as waiters and the meal was very successful.

When you are in your customer's country and are treated to a meal, it would be most respectful if you asked for a traditional restaurant of their local culture. That will potentially expose you to some strange cuisine and you must be prepared to indulge in their favorite dishes. Buying a guidebook will help you anticipate what you'll be experiencing.

I have often been asked on these occasions if there was anything I didn't like, and I normally respond that I'm not fond of liver but will eat almost anything. In fact, there are a number of items that I don't care for, but in trying to establish rapport with a customer, I watch my host and follow his example. Keeping in mind that all the dishes served are edible, even if not palatable, I eat what I'm offered. After some experience, you get to the point that you enjoy the opportunities to try new and exotic dishes.

Keep in mind that not too long ago the people of Southeast Asia thought the idea of drinking milk from an animal, such as a cow, was disgusting, though we consider it perfectly normal, tasty, and healthy. The same is true of many dishes throughout the world.

BUSINESS AND CULTURE

The issues that can cause the most grief to Americans are those relating directly to business practices.

WHEN TO GIVE

Gifts and gratuities are the rule in most counties, even when dealing with government officials. Whether these are considered bribes often depends on the perception of a witness, often a competitor. In the United States, the rules are clear. U.S. government representatives cannot accept any gift of any value, no matter how trivial. Many European countries now follow the same rules, and I've even encountered them in at least two countries in Southeast Asia. Some similar matters will be discussed in the next chapter.

That said, the practice of exchanging gifts is common throughout the world for non-government commercial business, and it can become quite expensive depending on the size of the project, the sizes of the companies involved, and the relative positions within their companies of the giver and the receiver of the gift. Types of gifts that I've found generally acceptable are golf items, such as gloves or packages of good golf balls, pen sets, and desk items. A current trend is a gift for the children of the customer. Your in-country partner or representative can provide advice on these matters, and your legal advisor can keep you out of trouble with the U.S. authorities and the I.R.S.

DIFFERENCES IN THE CLOCK

One other consideration, though not associated with customs, is the difference in time zones. Managing a project with an eight or nine-hour time difference, as between the West Coast of the United States and Europe, can be trying. When operating in Asia or the Middle East, the time difference can be a full twelve hours. Clearly, managing an international project is not a 9-to-5 proposition. All you can do is be aware and be prepared to operate on a whole new time cycle.

RECAPITULATION

There are four basic reasons for taking your company into the international marketplace:

1. Increase the profit potential of the company.
2. Provide for company growth.
3. Smooth out business cycles.
4. Extend the sales potential for existing products.

In spite of how small the world has become due to technology and transportation advances, customs in the international marketplace remain diverse and the manager of an international project must be sensitive to them. It is not his place to try to change customs, even those he finds offensive, but he can learn to appreciate most of the differences in the regions of the world and operate successfully within those differences.

There are differences that relate to race remaining in the world, and differences that relate to gender. There are differences to the time zones, and differences due to the selection of workdays.

Your age matters more in some parts of the world than others. Counterparts must often be near the same age.

Much of the world remains more formal than the United States. The use of a first name is a privilege not to be assumed but granted by the other person. There are protocols to the exchange of business cards and to formal communications between companies. It is important to honor and follow these protocols.

People who speak English as a second language tend to read and listen to English very carefully. The astute project manager will ensure that she writes and speaks with an equal amount of care.

Foreign business practices are often very different from those in the United States, and usually require that a personal relationship be built before a business relationship. The exchange of gifts is common, but to avoid giving too small or too large a gift, it is wise to have the advice of an in-country representative.

In the next chapter, I will describe some of the difficulties and risks associated with international projects. Though the reasons for going into international projects outweigh the arguments against it, those arguments must be taken into account.

Chapter 3

Difficulties and Risks of International Projects

Having looked at the reasons and the context for going international, it is necessary to look also at the downsides and risks associated with international projects. There are two major categories of risk. One is business, the other, political.

Business Competition

Competition in the United States can be brutal, but compared to that on the international scene, competition in this country is conducted in an environment of relative fairness. Internationally, there is likely to be a bias toward local or national businesses. When decisions are made about how the project will be divided, it is unlikely that American companies will even participate in the discussions.

In my experience, the American company must bring something to the project that isn't readily available in-country. This unique something may be substantive or it may be based on the local perception enhanced by your company's marketing department. Your local representative or your in-country partner can help during this first phase of the project—the early development of the project vision.

In Europe, as well as other parts of the world including the United States, companies form consortiums to compete for larger government projects. Often, there isn't even a competing consortium. The consortium divides the project among its members, and the only real competition is the effort to obtain a bigger piece of the pie as the project is divided.

There may be several tiers of companies involved, depending on the size of the project. At the highest level, the lead companies will likely form a corporation to manage the project for the consortium. The entire budget will be divided among this lead group. The second-tier companies are sub-contractors to the first tier and may include foreign companies, such as Americans. In recent years in Europe, I have rarely seen American companies successfully compete for the first tier, although it is possible to do so.

If yours is the only American company in the competition, the U.S. government has a number of agencies that can help. However, if more than one American company is involved in the competition, especially if they are competing against each other, the government will often remain at arm's length so as not to show any favoritism.

Forming a partnership with an in-country company, whether long-term or only for the duration of the project, is one of the best ways to improve your company's competitive position. Of course, the difficulty is in making the correct choice of a partner, since a bad choice will be worse than no partner at all. Finding a partner will take both time and research.

LEGAL ISSUES

A company accustomed to operating only in the United States will find itself in an unfamiliar legal environment outside the country. Sometimes the laws of the United States can be imposed, but normally those of the host country will apply to the contract. If the laws of the host country are imposed, it is especially important that the contract include arbitration in a neutral country—such as England—that has a history of legal fairness.

INCOTERMS (INternational COmmercial TERMS) is maintained by the International Chamber of Commerce as an international codification of terms used in international contracts. All countries now adhere to INCOTERMS for defining terms in contracts, making misunderstandings less common than they were a few years ago. INCOTERMS defines which party incurs which costs and at what point those costs are incurred. It does not have the force of law unless the contract refers to and imposes a specific dated version of the document, but its strength is that the definitions are the same in every language used. That makes the definition of the terms understood by all users of the document.

It would be a mistake to try to alter the terminology contained in INCOTERMS. It would give lawyers on both sides something to discuss for months—at your expense.

LABOR ISSUES

The fact that the laws of the host country apply to the contract does not relieve the American company of its duty to adhere to U.S. law. On occasion, the laws of the two countries will actually be in conflict, but in most cases, they will just be different.

> An example of one difference that can affect the profitability of a contract concerns the rights of labor. French law mandates a 35-hour workweek for each employee, salaried as well as hourly. This does not mean that employees can work as long as they want and just get paid for 35 hours. The law says they can work no more than 35 hours. The CEO of an offending firm can be fined heavily if anyone in his company violates the law. French law further stipulates that the company cannot pay the fine, the CEO must pay it personally.

If your plan calls for a 40-hour week, or longer, you will find that the project is likely to experience delays. Delays are deadly to profits.

TIME OFF

Another labor-related matter throughout Europe concerns the number of holidays and the lengths of paid vacations, which are far more generous than in the United States. There are national, regional, local, and religious holidays throughout the year. Also, most manufacturing plants and other businesses close for four weeks during the month of August, permitting the employees to take four of their standard six weeks of vacation during the continent's best weather. Often, the managers with whom you interface will not return to their offices until the second week in September, and will not receive visitors for another week or so.

Other long holidays to consider include Ramadan in Islamic countries and lunar New Year's in Asian countries. Ramadan lasts about 28 days (one lunar month), and News Year's celebrations typically last just over a week, depending on the day of the week the Chinese New Year falls. Little business can be conducted during those periods, so the astute businessperson plans it so that nothing critical is required during those times.

LAYOFFS

It is often quite expensive to release a European worker for any reason. In some countries, perhaps most, it will cost the employer at least two years salary and benefits. There will also be administrative costs and nonproductive delays involved in such a personnel action.

There are cost-effective ways to deal with these labor issues, but the company considering hiring foreign employees for overseas offices needs to think about it carefully and check the local laws.

There are in-country firms that will provide workers of any skill level, including engineers, to you for a fee. The worker remains an employee of that firm, and your company is relieved of the risks and burdens of a flexible workforce. The contract with the labor provider can be written in terms of staff-days of skill level or in terms of results expected.

CURRENCY ISSUES

Interest rates, inflation, and currency evaluations and variations are closely related. In the last 25 years, the United States has experienced a wide range of inflation and the interest rates that result. Other countries have similar problems, and the effects on the relative value of the currencies are complex. In general, however, if the customer country's inflation rate is higher than that of the United States, you can expect its currency to depreciate by an amount roughly equal to the differences in the two countries' inflation rates.

For purposes of project management, we are interested only in the resulting impact on currency exchange rates and in how to protect our company against losses as a result of those exchange rates, so a rigorous treatment of the subject is beyond the scope of this book. There is space, however, for a few comments to alert you to the importance of having someone monitor what's happening in the currency markets.

Currency variations can eliminate profits on an international project, and worse. Although the governments and the major trading banks of the world strive to maintain stability in the money markets, governments do devalue their currencies, exchange rates do swing unexpectedly and wildly, and economic changes do occur overnight. These are realities of the international marketplace that will affect the value of a contract.

There are several ways to protect a project from the uncertainties of exchange rates. The most common is to make your contracts payable in U.S. dollars. For short-term projects, that approach is acceptable to buyers. For longer projects, in which both the buyer and the seller are at risk, other approaches may be necessary.

A contract-defined exchange rate that reduces the risks to both parties is one approach. The defined rate would be one that is negotiated and accepted by both parties. It can be used if the currency of the buyer is on a downward or upward trend that is expected to continue for some time, and both parties agree that a change beyond the predetermined, contract-defined rate is unacceptable to one or both parties and is therefore a deal-stopper. That defined rate then becomes the exchange rate accepted by both parties.

Buying forward is another approach. This is much like buying futures in the commodity market, though in this case the commodity is money. Buying forward protects against future exchange rate variations. For the American seller or contractor, buying forward protects against a rising foreign currency value and assures that it gets the needed amount of whatever currency is used by the buyer. Large corporations commonly buy forward on contracts paid in foreign currency, so international banks are experts in the process.

The customer will often insist that payments be tied directly to achievement of specified critical milestones. When there is a payment attached, the agreement on completion criteria for that milestone becomes just as critical.

An alternative that reduces the risks for both parties, and even helps reduce other risks for the seller, is to include a large down payment and an accelerated payment schedule. With this approach there is often a rather severe penalty against the seller for late or non-performance on the project, so the negative factors have to be considered against the advantages.

MODIFYING PRODUCTS AND MARKETING MATERIAL

Most international projects will require some exporting of American-made goods, or goods that pass through the American system. In the example used later in this book, I demonstrate some of the difficulties that arise from exporting goods and services that would not occur on a purely domestic project.

This introduces four variables that must be considered:

1. The product.
2. The package.
3. The language.
4. The message.

There are many examples of products that have been successfully introduced into the global market with nothing changed but the language used in the message. There are many more examples of failures and embarrassment from this approach. However, if successful, it is the least expensive way to get a product to the international marketplace.

Most likely, some aspect of your product and service, its packaging, and its message will have to be modified. In one of my more successful projects, the customer wanted to use the product in a way not envisioned by my client company, using the basic hardware unchanged, converting the software to a different language on a different operating system, but maintaining the original functionality. The result was a significant improvement over the basic design and clear evidence that the product was suited to uses other than those originally considered. It was a classic win-win situation.

INCREASED ADMINISTRATIVE EXPENSES

There will be increases in expenses for phone and facsimile, mailings and courier services, different sizes of paper and envelopes to fit the overseas standard, legal reviews, regulatory reviews, and travel expenses. Packaging for overseas shipment by air or sea will differ from that shipped over land. There will be time delays in almost every transaction. For some, there will even be governmental reviews and fees for licenses. Insurance fees, bank charges, and expediter fees are other costs that have to be taken into account.

Travel costs are expensive but relatively predictable if the host country is overseas or even in South America, but hotel surcharges for telephones, faxes, business centers, and meeting rooms will run up the expenses. Other normal expenses to consider are rental cars and drivers where necessary, as well as rental of cell phones.

The time it takes to arrive at a signed contract in the international environment can be quite long. A government-sponsored project usually takes five years, but sometimes as many as 10. Much of that is spent in defining the project enough so that the responsible government entity can get funding authorization. The larger the project, the more time it seems to take to get to contract. Commercial projects tend to take less time because taking longer can cause a financial strain on both companies.

After the contract is won, there are the expenses of maintaining a core cadre of Americans in-country to manage and provide specialty services that might not be available there. The company's management will have to consider housing allowances, salary premiums, the extra expenses that families have merely because they are away from home or because they are separated, automobile allowances, exchange rate protection, and a host of other employee considerations.

There will be the expenses of maintaining an office in-country with a suite of business machines—computer, printer, fax machine, copier, filing cabinets, supplies, secretary, and administrative assistant. The machines can rarely be the same as those you've used in the U.S. Our machines are designed to operate on 110 volts at 60 hertz. Most other countries use 220 volts at 50 hertz. Even videotape players are different. They use a recording standard that is incompatible with our machines.

ON TIME PAYMENTS

Although most experiences will be positive, it would not be correct to say there won't be problems in this area. While customers generally pay in accordance with the contract, there have been bad experiences in Africa, Asia, and the Middle East.

Even when the customer pays in accordance with the contract, there may be difficulties. First, though the customer authorizes payments on time and in accordance with the contract, sometimes the host government will delay transfer of funds for up to 60 days. They do this through the banks by not allowing hard currency transactions to take place until they have been reviewed by a government agency.

The second difficulty has to do with the contract. During negotiations, criteria for payment milestones will have been agreed upon. You can be certain that members of the customer management team and their legal advisors will search the contract thoroughly to find a reason not to pay or to delay payment. That reason—something the contractor has done or failed to do that would put it in violation of the terms—will often relate to formal communication requirements. In international business, as I have said and will reiterate, the documentation must be precise. The customer will force the contractor to abide by the letter of the contract without any regard to oral agreements to the contrary.

Those two cautions aside, international as well as American companies want to avoid costly legal action or arbitration and will abide by the terms of the contract without serious challenge. This is not to say, though, that they won't take advantage of any gaps in your knowledge of the terms of the contract.

A common approach to payments that assures both that the supplier gets paid and that the buyer's requirements are met is the use of letters of credit. With a letter of credit, the bank selected determines when the requirements for payment have been met and issues the funds to the seller. The banks charge a fee for this service, but it is an effective way to assure payment. There is a need to be precise in every entry on the form, however, since the bank will insist that the written requirement is met exactly.

An example of how precise the wording must be on a letter of credit concerns PepsiCola. That company's Russian supplier of vodka suffered a lengthy delay in bank authorization of payment because the letter of credit specified that the Port of Los Angeles was the delivery port. However, a Longshoreman strike at Los Angeles caused the ship to be diverted to San Francisco. Since the paperwork no longer matched, the bank refused payment.

The major part of the work of international banking has been to reduce risks in international transactions by issuing letters of credit, by selling and buying forward exchange contracts, and by other methods.

Though the legal basis for it is unclear, bank issuance of letters of credit has a long history. It is accepted throughout the world that banks have this power, though not always authorized by legislative actions. Section 13 of the Federal Reserve Act grants member banks the power to accept drafts drawn on them. Acceptance indicates that banks will pay the drafts on specified dates. The courts have ruled that the power to issue letters of credit stating that drafts would be honored may be implied. Since 1913, there has been no question of the power of Fed member banks, and all national banks, to issue letters of credit. Travelers' checks are a form of letter of credit but in international business transactions they are called commercial documentary letters of credit, because drafts are honored only when they are presented along with specified documents in proper form on the proper date.

The major risk faced by exporters is that governments may impose restrictions that prevent payment. With a letter of credit, exporters are assured of payment if they meet the conditions of the letter of credit. The risk is effectively eliminated, and cases in which governments have interfered are few. There are even means of honoring these instruments in the event of war.

Importers are also protected in that the exporter will not be paid unless the conditions have been met. These conditions might include certificates of quantity, quality, and other criteria established between the parties. The bank verifies *documentation*, not product, so the system depends on the honesty of the parties.

Letters of credit are normally irrevocable up to a specified date without prior notice to beneficiaries. This protects both parties to the exchange.

Participation of a government agency like the Export-Import Bank may be advantageous. Interest rates are lower and the agency may even provide part of the total loan financing and even accepting a later repayment to permit earlier repayment to banks.

THE ROLE OF THE PROJECT MANAGER

It is important that the project manager be a key player in contract negotiations. In my experience, and that of my colleagues, when the project manager did not participate in formulating the contract, the project suffered in terms of both profit and customer satisfaction—and the project manager suffered in terms of career advancement. This is another example of poor early planning.

EXPORT LICENSES AND TECHNICAL ASSISTANCE AGREEMENTS

Although the events in the early 1990s in Europe and the former Soviet Union have resulted in significant easing of U.S. and multilateral export controls on west-east trade, the events of September 11, 2001, as well as developments in many other areas of the world, have underscored the importance of nonproliferation controls on weapon technology. The Department of Commerce's Bureau of Industry and Security has responded by focusing attention on commodities, technology, software and services that could be used to develop or deliver weapons of mass destruction. New regulations were published in 1991 that place greater emphasis on the end-use or end-user of exported items.

Up to 1991 and the President's Enhanced Proliferation Control Initiative (EPCI), license requirements were identified and validated by checking the items and country of destination against the Commerce Control List (CCL). An item that was not on the CCL could in most cases be exported under a general license. Under the new EPCI controls, the end-use and end-user have become critical in determining whether an export requires a validated license.

The CCL is found in Supplement 1 to Section 799.1 of the Export Administration Regulations. Supplement 2 contains the General Terminology Note and General Software Note, which are necessary to understand certain technology and software entries in the CCL. For most commercial products, companies will deal with the Department of Commerce. Companies new to the import/export business will need a licensing expert to advise them. Often your international bank manager can help, but I advise that you obtain the services of an import-export management company.

While licenses are no longer required for all exports, they are required for those restricted items listed in the *Export Administration Regulations (EAR)*. Items are listed by country, and those items marked by an "X" for a specific country may require a license or an exception prior to export. Advice can be obtained from the Department of Commerce at the following address:

> Department of Commerce/Bureau of Industry and Security
> Office Exporting Licensing/Export Counseling Division
> 14th Street and Pennsylvania Avenue, N.W.
> Room H1099D
> Washington, D.C. 20230

Not all restricted items are listed in the EAR. Those items that fall under other departments and agencies are subject to the regulations and control of those government organizations. Some of those agencies are:

- Federal Trade Commission for information on "Made in USA" labeling requirements, standards, and competition.

- Food and Drug Administration.

- Office of Foreign Asset Controls of the U.S. Treasury Department.

- Office of Defense Trade Controls of the U.S. Department of State, which controls defense related exports.

- U.S. Customs Service helps exporters with Export Declarations and other exporter information.

- U.S. Department of State.

- Nuclear Regulatory Commission governs exports of nuclear equipment and materials.

- Department of Energy controls exports of natural gas and electric power.

- Drug Enforcement Agency controls exports of narcotics and dangerous drugs, including prescription drugs.

- Bureau of Alcohol, Tobacco, and Firearms controls the export of alcohol and cigarettes, and the temporary export of firearms. Permanent export of firearms is controlled by the Department of State.

- Department of Agriculture controls the export of certain food items

- Department of Interior controls exports of endangered fish and wildlife, migratory birds, and bald and golden eagles.

The U.S. Congress has listed three reasons for exercising control over exports from the United States. In the most general terms, they are:

- National security.

- Foreign policy.

- Short supply.

If a product or software that originated outside the United States was modified even trivially by a U.S. company, it may fall into the category of technology export, and it and the technical data associated with it will fall under the control of the Department of State.

POLITICAL ISSUES

The political factor must be considered early in selecting a market for your business efforts. Newspapers and international news programs on television offer an early indication of the political risks in various parts of the world. This information will naturally affect where you decide to place your energies. If it looks as though the political environment creates too large a business risk or puts your employees at danger, that region should be rejected for most products and services—unless, of course, that's the business you're in.

The fact that the political situation in an otherwise stable country can turn sour after the project has gotten underway represents a serious financial risk to the company. The revolt in Iran in 1979, though information was available to make it foreseeable, caught many U.S. defense contractors by surprise and cost them millions of dollars in abandoned equipment and cancelled contracts.

Work can come to a halt due to temporary periods of instability or even long labor actions. Work stoppages naturally cost a project heavily. Some countries are known for frequent strikes. Italy, for example, has numerous strikes every year, but they are usually planned and announced in advance and last only a day or so. This is not an unstable situation because it can be anticipated in the project plan.

> Other political issues are more serious. One company was forced to bring their entire project crew home from Israel due to the sudden instability in that region in late 1999, bringing its project to a complete halt for a long period at great cost to both the company and the government of Israel. The 1973 war stopped everything for three to four months and resulted in considerable additional expense to the Government of Israel to compensate the contractor for much of his losses.

Much of the political risk can be mitigated through terms in the contract. When contracting to operate in regions of potential insecurity, include terms, such as force majeure clauses, that relieve you as contractor from penalties and other costs. If you are not successful in negotiating terms that protect the company, walk away from that business to other markets.

All risks of any nature can become business risks but once you choose a geographic area of relative stability in which to market your products and services, you can turn your attention to the purely business risks of the venture.

Forming a partnership with an in-country company, whether long-term or only for the duration of the project, is one of the best ways to improve your company's competitive position. Of course, the difficulty is in making the correct choice of a partner, since a bad choice will be worse than no partner at all. Take the time to do the research properly.

RECAPITULATION

The risks associated with international projects are generally either business or political. First, there is a strange new competitive environment, which will usually favor a national company over the American firm, and consortiums are formed that exclude foreign involvement at their highest levels.

Labor issues in European countries, as well as some others, can be cause for concern due to the protections afforded labor by laws against layoffs and other discharges. The large number of holidays and extensive vacation and sick leave allowances can increase the cost of labor beyond the original plans if they are not taken into account.

The legal environment will be unfamiliar. In-country representatives and subcontractors can help you avoid unnecessary legal difficulties.

As the currencies of the world fluctuate among each other, these fluctuations, if large in the country of interest, can affect the profit of an international project. There are ways to avoid these risks—contracting in U.S. dollars, defining exchange rates in the contract, buying forward, and negotiating favorable payment terms.

Your products may have to be modified for the target country, your promotion and marketing materials will surely have to be modified to enter the foreign markets, and the advertising will have to be changed.

Administrative costs will go up as a result of entering the international market. Travel costs may be the largest increase, but numerous other expenses will also rise.

There are ways to ensure that payments are made on time, such as letters of credit and contracted payment terms.

Export licenses may be required, depending on the product to be exported. A number of government agencies have an interest in these licenses, among them the U.S. Departments of State, Commerce, and Agriculture. Special licenses may be required for technology transfer and software products.

The political situation in the target country must be considered early in the planning phase to avoid getting into a situation that you must later extract yourself from with probable loss of profit. Though the political situation in some countries can turn bad quickly, catching firms by surprise, normally there is ample warning of countries it would be well to avoid.

CHAPTER 4
THE GROUNDWORK

Now that you have evaluated the pros and cons of going international with your business and made the decision to continue, the next step is to take a look at some resources that might help you. The first question owners and managers usually ask is, "How do we get started?" The problems seem huge. Typically, the company doesn't have a presence in the target country and no one on staff speaks the language. Are there places to turn for help? The answer, of course, is yes, and the questions will be answered in this chapter.

The most common errors firms make as they begin to export products and services, according to the Small Business Administration, are:

- Failure to plan or to have in place a master strategy for the international marketplace.

- Lack of commitment by top management.

- Poor selection of overseas representatives and distributors.

- Lack of focus on specific countries or regions.

- Lack of attention to the international market when domestic sales return to normal.

- Failure to treat international relationships with the same respect as domestic relationships.

- Assuming that a approach that is successful in one country will also work in another.

- Failure to modify products to meet local cultural preferences or regulations.

- Failure to print brochures, service agreements, warranties, and other common documents in the local language.

- Failure to use outside experts when the firm cannot afford its own export department.

- Failure to consider alternatives, such as licensing and joint ventures, to overcome import restrictions, limited production capacity, or resource limitations.

- Failure to provide follow-up service after sales.

A haphazard approach to the international market will most certainly be doomed from the start, just as it would be in the domestic market. The best opportunities will be missed, costs will increase to an unacceptable level, and the company can be misled into abandoning potentially lucrative international business altogether. Doing the research and formulating an international business strategy based on facts and careful analysis increases the chance that the best options will be chosen, resources will be used efficiently, and the effort will be successful.

The primary purpose of an international business plan is to assemble facts, constraints, and assumptions in order to create an action statement for the business. The statement will include specific attainable objectives, time schedules, and milestones so that success can be measured.

Before the first overseas steps are made, there are decisions the directors of the company must make—time and money commitments, personnel to dedicate to the effort. Upper management has to be committed to making international business a success and it has to maintain this commitment even after the domestic market for its products and services return to normal. Business cycles repeat. It is not wise to abandon your markets and then have to start all over to break back into the international marketplace.

A good example of this type of commitment is one of my most successful projects. I was hired to manage a program that was described during my interviews as "imminent." However, imminent turned out to be not so soon. It took just over three years before the contract was signed and work began. Those three years were spent traveling back and forth to Italy, writing and rewriting the proposal, pricing and repricing the effort to fit the customer's budget, and finally preparing the contract word by word. At the end of the contract period the company was quite happy with the profits, but it took the confidence and commitment of upper management to hold on for those three years and give the project time to succeed.

DOING THE PEOPLE WORK

To achieve strong upper management support, the project manager has to prepare the groundwork thoroughly. He has to convince the directors of the company that (1) this is a solid opportunity with relatively low risk and (2) he has the knowledge base, the staff, and the requisite resources to bring the project to a profitable conclusion. How to gain this support is covered more completely in the next chapter on preparing a game plan.

Also, later in the book, there is advice on how to select overseas representatives (Chapter 6) and foreign subcontractors (Chapter 11). First, though, the project manager must establish the criteria and the role to be played by the in-country representative and ensure that the candidate selected can and will fulfill those responsibilities. Too often, the in-country representative is chosen based solely on a self-proclaimed list of important contacts. Getting rid of a bad representative can be expensive. It is better to spend the time and money to choose wisely.

There are several approaches to the international market and the company and project managers must be open to new ideas.

For the example used in this book, I take a plausible though fictional approach that was based loosely on one of my own experiences. To begin with, we assumed our company was in the business of building factories and office structures, and we used some of the approaches recommended in this chapter to find a customer. After some months, we still hadn't found any interest in our services.

Over dinner, one of our contacts suggested we give some thought to one of his clients who wanted to build a "very special log cabin." We advised him that is not our strength. We work in steel, not wood, and with businesses, not individuals, we insisted. He told us, though, that this was a very wealthy man who requires a secure and private place to protect him and his family from people who might do them harm.

After some thought and discussion among our team, we decided we could do it and make a profit, so we pursued the idea further and presented it to our management back in the States.

My father once told me that people don't buy from companies, they buy from people. That is certainly valid advice for the international marketplace. You cannot just walk into a company overseas, present your card, and ask to be placed on the bidders list for projects. Managers and officers of foreign companies want to establish a relationship with you, to become friends, before they offer to do business. At the time you begin to establish a relationship, you may have little idea of what business might be available, and no idea at all of the project you may be ultimately be asked to bid on. But you'll be in on the planning of the project at the early stages and will help shape the final product.

In fact, if the first you've heard of the project is just before the request for proposal is released, you will have no more than a minute chance of winning, even with the best proposal at the best price. Still, your proposal may be of value to the customer—who will use it as leverage in negotiating better terms for those on the company short list.

It's true that there are times when a customer from another country appears at your doorstep with a request that you prepare a specific proposal. He has heard of your company—perhaps through your Internet site or another customer—and wants you to do the job for him. That's not so rare as it may sound, but not so common that you can count on it if you're trying to break into the international scene.

FINDING CUSTOMERS

The task of finding a customer can be overwhelming with the whole world as a market, but there are governmental and commercial organizations in the business of providing help. Customers, as always, can come from the most unexpected directions, such as:

U.S. GOVERNMENT SOURCES

Our government is huge, and the resources it provides are many and varied. Among the departments and agencies dedicated to helping businesses and fostering exports of products, services and technologies are:

- *U.S. Small Business Administration.* If your company employs fewer than 500 people and has annual revenues of less than $50 million, it fits the government's definition of a small business and can use the huge amount of information available from the SBA subjects ranging from how to start a business to how to export its products. The Web site is *www.sba.gov.* Click on Business Opportunities or International Trade for several information-rich links and even some on-line training. The three organizations within the SBA most relevant to our efforts are:

1. SCORE (Service Corps of Retired Executive). SCORE is a national organization of more than 13,000 volunteers, experienced business executives who provide free counseling, workshops, and seminars to small businesses and start-ups. Many of them have international experience.

2. SBDCs (Small Business Development Centers). The SBA sponsors SBDCs in partnership with state and local governments, the educational community, and the private sector. They offer counseling, training, and research assistance on all aspects of small business management .

3. SBI (Small Business Institute). SBI provides intensive management counseling from business students supervised by faculty. They can be very helpful in finding the best foreign market for a particular product or service.

• *U.S. Department of Commerce.* For companies of all sizes, the Department of Commerce is the primary source of information on international business. Commerce supports exports and efforts to export, though it provides little assistance for importers. Its Internet site, *www.doc.gov*, should be the first stop for any company looking for market opportunities outside the United States. Of the many subordinate organizations within Commerce, the following three are most important for our purposes:

1. ITA (International Trade Administration). ITA's international trade specialists help locate the best foreign markets for your product or service. This is the most important contact for a company just getting into exporting—and when you take on an international project, you are certainly exporting services, probably goods, and very likely technology. The Web site, *www.ita.doc.gov*, contains information on current business opportunities, trade events, trade development initiatives, and demographics.

2. DECs (District Export Councils). Members of a typical DEC are banks, manufacturers, law offices, trade associations, government offices, and educational institutions. They educate, counsel, and guide businesses in their individual marketing needs. They primarily serve small businesses.

3. US&FCS (United States and Foreign Commercial Service). The commercial service helps U.S. firms compete effectively in the global marketplace. It has trade specialists throughout the world. It provides information on international markets, agents and distributors, trade leads, business opportunities, trade barriers, and prospects abroad.

• *U.S. Department of Agriculture.* The Foreign Agricultural Service (FAS) within the Department of Agriculture can obtain specific market information for agricultural products. The USDA's Web site is *www.usda.gov* and FAS's is *www.fas.usda.gov*.

PRIVATE SOURCES

In the private sector, there is a great deal of help for companies expanding into the international market. Among these are:

- *Exporters' associations, such as:*
  1. World Trade Centers. The 300 or so World Trade Centers in 100 countries publish newsletters, provide meeting rooms and trade libraries, and can help with hotel reservations and other needs of the business traveler.

  2. The American Association of Exporters and Importers provides a liaison with the U.S. government. It publishes regular updates on regulatory matters affecting international business.

  3. The Small Business Exporters Association, along with a number of other groups, can assist in international market research.

- *Trade associations, including:*
  1. The National Federation of International Trade Associations lists more than 150 organizations in the U.S. that help the small business owner enter international markets.

  2. The Telecommunications Industry Association is typical of the over 5,000 trade and professional association currently operating in the United States that promote international trade activities for their members.

  3. Chambers of Commerce often employ international trade specialists who gather information on markets abroad, or have international trade committees willing to help members. I have belonged to three different chambers and each has had an international committee of members with experience in international business affairs.

FOREIGN EMBASSIES AND CONSULATES

Each country interested in doing business with the United States stations officials in this country to assist. Many have Web sites. In all cases, they are, like our own government, interested primarily in exporting to the United States, but they can be an invaluable source of information on business in their own country.

IN-COUNTRY REPRESENTATIVES

Your own in-country representative, whether an employee of your company or a colleague who is a local national, can help you find and evaluate business opportunities.

In-country representatives are often American expatriates, some coming from families that immigrated to the United States from the target country. Often they are local residents who have studied in America. Thus, they know and understand the languages and customs on both sides of the ocean. However, this alone may not be enough

A long time manager of an office in Italy who was an American citizen spoke Italian as fluently as a native. He also had contacts at all levels of the government and with many large corporations. He seemed the perfect person for our project. But the customer would not discuss his company's sensitive business information with our representative in the room. My team naively thought it was due to his facility with the language—he could listen in on discussions among the Italians. During drinks after dinner one evening, my counterpart suggested that the man drew two salaries—a clear reference to inappropriate behavior. A company investigation ensued, the allegation was confirmed, and our representative's employment was terminated.

Because soliciting business from the entire world requires resources beyond all but the largest corporations, company resources must be directed to specific countries or regions. Research into potential markets will let you evaluate trade-offs between market areas so that management can decide where its resources will bring the best return on investment.

When it is time to expand the international market into additional countries, further research will be required because the approach used in the initial international markets undoubtedly must be changed for the new markets. Nor will the products and services offered successfully in one market necessarily be as well accepted in the new target.

For the purposes of example, I created the country of Europistania. It is like a former Soviet Bloc country, with a majority population of Muslims, a large minority of Christians, and a small minority of Jews. The government is democratic, with a parliament, but several powerful families have influence over the actions of the government. Our ideal in-country manager should be an American citizen whose family recently immigrated to the United States. After some discussion, we have decided that his religion is not important. We will expand on this starting in the next chapter.

RECAPITULATION

Among the many errors made by companies trying to enter the international market, most relate to lack of commitment and failure to treat the international customer as well as the domestic customer. Another large group of errors reflects an assumption that all customers are alike, whatever their country or region, and the marketing approaches that worked in one area will work in another.

Going international must be carefully planned. What will be involved in the move, the constraints imposed, and the assumptions relating to the approach have to be considered. There must be milestones to be met, attainable goals, and time schedules so that progress can be measured.

Most important, upper management must be committed to international business over the long term, including the periods in which the domestic business is more profitable. The cycles will reverse, and the company that maintains its commitments will benefit when they do.

Using the resources listed in this chapter will facilitate your search for a customer, but you still have to do the actual work.

The next chapter introduces the game plan. The game plan is a living document that will guide company activities through the marketing phase and into the contract phase, where it transitions into the integrated master plan for the project.

Chapter 5
The Game Plan

Most troubled projects, international as well as domestic, can trace the source of their problems back to a poor game plan. In the eagerness for action, planning is too often given inadequate attention, so the project's game plan is not well thought through. To make matters worse, in these situations, it is then often poorly executed.

The purpose of the game plan is to dissect the prospective project from beginning to end, reduce the risks, and anticipate all the activities required to bring the project to fruition. When its primary purpose is just to get through management briefings for corporate approval of the effort or to simply provide the marketer's ideas of how to capture the business, it will be of little value to the project manager, or anyone else.

Preparing a thorough, effective game plan will prevent many problems and help mitigate risks. A good game plan is a living document that guides the project's efforts all the way from the beginning marketing effort to the final day of the project, updated on a regular basis as it matures. Accordingly, it is a document kept in the project room to be read and reviewed regularly, keeping the project on track and the plan viable. This is a tall order, but not only can it be done, it must be done.

Much of the game plan depends on the type of contract you're seeking. Here are a number of different contract types in international business:

- The most common for commercial projects is *firm fixed price (FFP),* in which the price negotiated, taking into account incentives and penalties, is the final price to be paid. The contractor must try to make a profit from that value.

- Another type, rarely used today, is the *cost-plus contract,* in which the customer assumes the cost risks and the contractor is guaranteed a percentage profit. These were common in the defense industry for developmental projects in which the government assumed all risks, until they fell out of favor because of notoriously extravagant cost overruns.

- *Cost-plus-incentive-fee (CPIF)* is now more common on developmental projects. It is like the cost-plus contract but has more controls and incentives for keeping costs low.

There are variations of these basic types, such as FPI (fixed-price-incentive), but most commercial projects operate under an FFP contract with penalties and incentives.

A project is like a subordinate business of the company. It must make a profit to be successful, just like the parent company, so it needs a business plan. The basic elements of the game plan are:

- Description of the project.

- Marketing plan.

- Description and analysis of the competition and the competitive environment.

- Description of how the project will be performed.

- List of key personnel and why each is important to the effort.

- Financial data, including customer's budget information, if possible.

The game plan may cover more elements than these basics, and it can assume any format that facilitates its use, but it is important that it be prepared in a form that can be understood by all team members who have a stake in any portion of the project. It may not be appropriate, for example, to distribute complete financial data to all team members, but they will all need the sections on project description and the project manager's vision of how the project will be performed. While it is best to share information, there are situations where it is impractical or even inappropriate.

PROJECT DESCRIPTION

In the early stages, the description of the project may be short and simple: "The project is to build an American log cabin on a hillside in the country of Europistania." (Don't try to look *that* up in your world atlas). Later, as more information is available, details of size, time, exact location, purpose, and how it will be built can be added.

The section describing the project is important. It sets out the scope of the job, what it includes, and perhaps most important, what it does not include. When your spouse says he wants to retile the bathroom, it is significant to know that he meant the tub, shower, and counter, but not the floor. All the team members, the company management, the subcontractors, and the customer have to agree that the project to be performed is properly described in this section. The better you all understand the project, the better the goals will be understood, and the fewer disagreements you will have with the customer and your own superiors. This section is the guide for the rest of the document.

There is a significant difference in projects that require you to develop hardware or software and those that can incorporate only off-the-shelf equipment and software. The approaches, the organization, and the skills of the staff chosen will thus be influenced by the description of the project. The hybrid project, one that takes off-the-shelf packages and assembles them into a new product, is more like developmental than a totally "rack and stack" off-the-shelf project. In fact, adapting any product to a new function will be more developmental than is obvious at first look. Making errors at the description stage will compound the problems and costs later in the project.

In my experience, the buyer is usually able to describe what he wants only in nontechnical, general terms. The contractor has to take the responsibility to define the project in technical terms to elicit more precise understanding of the scope of the work. Though this is common in the domestic market, it assumes a different scale overseas. It is part of the project manager's job to apply technical expertise to defining project specifications from the buyer's more general description of what is wanted.

Converting a general description into specifications and gaining the customer's acceptance, buy-in, can take months. Each adjustment may require a new budget estimate and may affect contract negotiations progressing in parallel with the project description.

Depending on your company's organization and size, the marketing staff, rather than the management group, may be responsible for the project during these early phases. Whether the group is called marketing, business development, front end of the business, or some other term intended to define their role, in my experience the project manager must be actively involved. It is a mistake to wait until the definition is set before selecting a manager to run the project. Leaving the project manager out of any part of project development, especially for international efforts, can be the seed of later troubles with the customer.

THE MARKETING PLAN

A marketing plan spells out the goals, strategies, and means that will be used to establish a strong competitive position and win the project. The marketing plan describes the strategy for winning the project and ensuring that the customer is satisfied.

The key to the marketing plan is the customer. Prepare your message in terms that demonstrate a benefit to the customer. Instead of telling the customer what you do, describe how she benefits from what you do. Too often, the strategy is to sell the company's products and services, and the only customer focus is an attempt to convince her that those products and services are what she needs. The strategy starts with the company, and makes full circle back to the company without stopping to consider on the customer's needs. This is clearly a poor marketing strategy.

Find out first what the customer's needs are, how he values certain attributes of products and services, and then decide how to present or adapt what you have to what he needs. Instead of "This is what I have and why you need it," you're saying, "I understand your problems and needs and this is how I can satisfy them." An additional benefit to thinking in terms of the customer's needs is that you may quickly become aware that your company doesn't have a reasonable chance of winning the project and you can divert the resources that would otherwise be wasted to another project.

It should be clear that the marketing plan discussed here is not the corporate strategic marketing plan, though both should be consistent with each other.

The best way to start preparing a marketing plan is to use the S.W.O.T. analysis—identify strengths, weaknesses, opportunities, and threats. Strengths and weaknesses are factors internal to your company and the project; opportunities and threats are generally external factors. You will use this analysis many times throughout the planning cycle.

First, be realistic about the strengths your company and your staff bring to the project. Many of what you may consider unique strengths are often characteristics shared by your competitors. One way to approach this is to identify the one best reason a customer should choose your company over a competitor. After that, identify the next best reason and so on. This will give you a short but relevant list. Your marketing strategy must then emphasize that one best reason *for this customer.*

Then look at your company's weaknesses from the viewpoint of a customer or a competitor. Identify the one thing about your company that the competitor is going to try to capitalize on—your employees may have a better idea of that than your managers. Identify as many weaknesses as you can and list them in order of seriousness.

In your communications with the customer, you will want to emphasize your strengths and minimize your weaknesses. Sometimes you may have to own up to certain weaknesses; if so, you need to have something to offer that will mitigate those drawbacks. Don't let them just sit there with nothing to neutralize them—your competitor will seize upon that as an opportunity.

You must review opportunities and threats regularly. You will be looking for opportunities to expand your business and improve its profit picture
daily.

Opportunities seem difficult to identify for the typical project manager
busy with the day-to-day activities of the project, trying to respond to customer communications, and answering to the many internal company
demands. However, the in-country representative is in an excellent position
to identify new customers, to know when a competitor may be dropping
out, to see a chance to enhance the current project, or to spot other opportunities that arise during the course of the project.

Threats are everywhere. The project manager must be quick to identify each new risk. The preliminary analysis will concentrate only on external events that can adversely impact the project, such as a challenge to the
funding levels approved by the customer, a new competitor with a unique
capability, the approaching obsolescence of your own product, developmental problems, underestimating the scope of work, a disagreement in the
meaning of an article in the contract or the statement of work, or possible
cancellation of the project for political reasons.

The threats you have identified will be part of your risk analysis and
should be dealt with in your risk management system.

You will present both opportunities and threats to your own management to help them evaluate the status and value of the whole project.

ANALYSIS OF THE COMPETITION

Often your customer will tell you about the strong points of your competitors, but you can't always trust the information your customer provides.
The customer has his own agenda; preservation of your company's profits
isn't necessarily part of it.

Information on competitors can be gained via market intelligence. Be
careful to stay within legal and ethical bounds when gathering intelligence,
especially when you're working on U.S. government-sponsored projects. If
you acquire information about a competitor that your company is not
authorized to have, you have the legal obligation to inform both the competitor and your customer that you possess the information and how you
got it.

In some cases, possession of the information will disqualify your company and could be cause for legal action. In 1996, Boeing and Lockheed were competing to become the primary maker of rockets for launching U.S. government satellites. Boeing won the competition, but a former Lockheed employee who worked for Boeing during the competitive phase was accused of providing documents to his new employer about Lockheed's approach. Senior managers at Boeing had already ordered the documents returned and fired the employee, but the ensuing court battles, and potential sanctions by the government through independent actions, had—and continue to have—the potential of damaging the reputation and fortunes of Boeing by suspending some of the military work that is so important to the success of the company.

The legal ramifications are not as strict when you're dealing with foreign competition for an international project, but rules of ethics still apply. It may seem that the ethics applied by your competitor are not the same as those you try to follow, but it is prudent to maintain your company's integrity in all matters. The companies that survive the longest tend to make decisions based on principle. To do otherwise may result in short-term gains but places too many risks in the path of the long-term success of the company. Consider the case of Enron.

The competition, and often the customer, will also gather information about your company. The competitor will seek information on your proposal and price, and the customer will want to know how the price he's asked to pay compares with how much similar projects performed by your company cost. This type of information is considered proprietary; you must protect it from inadvertent release. Mark all papers that contain proprietary information, and be sure to maintain control of the means used to transmit it. People have bragged to me that they can get a copy of anything sent to a hotel via fax for less than $50. Though unethical, even illegal, it happens. You must know who is receiving the information and how they will use and protect it. Never fax proprietary information to an unattended fax machine. Use a shredder before tossing anything in the trash. While the competition may well be bound by the ethics of fair play, constant vigilance should be the norm.

The competition can also profit from the carelessness of members of the project team and other company employees. A few years ago, I was sitting in the business lounge of a hotel in Seoul, Korea, that is popular with American businesspeople, when the hostess announced a phone call for someone I knew was vice president of another company. We were not working the same project, but because he carried on his conversation in the lounge instead of having the call transferred to his room, I learned all the pertinent details of a proposal he was making to a customer while I read the newspaper nearby. His competitors often used the same hotel and likely overheard the same conversation. He was clueless when it came to protecting proprietary information.

People are especially careless with cell phone conversations. They will discuss the most private matters in public, unaware that their voices travel beyond the mouthpiece of the phone. The next time you're at an airport lounge or in a mall, just listen in on a few people talking on cell phones.

There are other means of gathering information available about the competition: Business journals, newspapers, magazine articles, catalogs, annual reports, and other public sources allow you to postulate your competitive position with enough accuracy for you to capitalize on your own strengths and the weaknesses of competitors.

Following are the eight pieces of information you want to know about each of your competitors:

1. *The nature of the business.* Size, annual sales, names of officers, and breadth of product lines and services.

2. *Strengths.* Its reputation in the industry in the area that intersects with your company's activities.

3. *Weaknesses.* Areas your own marketing package can point out to your advantage.

4. *History of on-time performance* on previous contracts, particularly in the host country.

5. *Previous relationships with the customer*, if any. A long history with the customer will give a competitor a distinct advantage.

6. T*he competitive playing field.* Is it level and fair? In international business, it is rarely either. Every company wants a fair competition in which it enjoys an unfair advantage. Some rules may give

your competitor an advantage; in the United States, under certain circumstances, identified classes of business are granted a legal advantage over competitors of other classifications.

7. *Subcontracting opportunities.* Some countries divide contracts among in-country competing companies, allowing each to partner with outside firms for technical expertise within their own portion of the contract. Consortiums are common in Europe. Often, positioning your company as a subcontractor to the partner provides an excellent position for a successful project.

8. *Potential as an in-country partner.* In-country partners can provide many advantages to an American company, especially as an instant source of local knowledge in all areas of the business.

It is legal and ethical to acquire all this information. Any other information you get about a competitor that is or should have been protected must raise a question about to your obligation to return it.

HOW THE PROJECT WILL BE PERFORMED

This section is the project manager's concept of how the effort will be conducted. It provides guidelines for the master plan and the master schedule. It should have enough detail that subordinate managers can plan their own activities consistent with it.

This section covers those aspects of the job that will be performed by both U.S. and in-country subcontractors or partners, identifying the point of contact for the other firms. Identify any design reviews and management reviews that must be scheduled and who will be responsible.

A top-level schedule, such as a Gantt or PERT chart, must be shown as well as penalties for missing scheduled delivery dates. The section will describe the risk management system, methods for measuring and reporting progress against schedule and budget, and any software packages that will be used as management tools.

This is also a good place to define the timing of project management meetings and the format expected for reports expected. For all but very small projects, a weekly meeting with the project manager in which the staff reports progress is about the right frequency. Daily meetings with certain members of the staff or about emerging problem areas might be appropriate. In the most general terms, the questions to which the project manager wants answers from staff are:

• The status of the budget and schedule for each area.

• Accomplishments versus promises for the previous week.

• Status of anticipated risks and mitigation efforts in each area.

• Emerging problems likely to require management attention.

• Next week's plans.

Use meeting techniques: Publish an agenda, fix a time limit for each presentation, ensure that everyone arrives on time, insist that everyone come prepared, and publish minutes. Meetings are a necessary medium of management but unless they are conducted efficiently, they will cost more than they benefit.

KEY PERSONNEL AND THEIR ROLES

In the next chapter the means of organizing the project, including the people working on it, are discussed in detail but, clearly, every project demands a skill set. The project manager must define the skill set that will be required to complete the project on time and within budget, then use this as a benchmark against which to identify the personnel she needs to work the program, whether she has to hire from outside or can draw on personnel already employed by the company. One method of doing this is shown in Figure 5.1.

By cross-matching skills needed against personnel tentatively selected for the project, as in Figure 5.1, you can make logical staffing decisions. For instance, in the figure, there are two skills needed, C and J. that are not available within the company, so other individuals will have to be identified to fill those needs. Also, both Bob and Allen possess Skills A and B, but Allen also possesses G. It may be possible to replace Bob with someone who possesses the missing skills, unless the demands of Skills A and B are such that you need both Bob and Allen.

FIGURE 5.1
SAMPLE SKILLS CROSS-REFERENCE CHART

Skills	***Staff Available***				
Needed	***Bob R.***	***Allen J.***	***Pat K***	***Carol D.***	***Frank B.***
Skill A	X	X			X
Skill B	X	X			
Skill C					
Skill D			X		
Skill E				X	
Skill F				X	
Skill G		X			
Skill H					X
Skill J					

A third dimension to the chart that isn't shown is the element of time—the points in the project schedule when a given skill is needed and when it is no longer needed. Later, you will see how to add this element to your planning.

The figure is a simple depiction of what can be a hugely complex job on a large project, but no matter how big the project, the effort must be made so that the project staffing profile is efficient.. Another benefit of the process is that precisely defining the skills required for the job and the timing of the need for each of the skills significantly helps the planning process as a whole.

If the company employs a matrix-style organization, timing the need for specific skills and individuals will be absolutely necessary if the functional organization is to provide efficient support of the project.

FINANCIAL DATA

Later chapters describe the use of financial controls to help manage the project. Though the financial data required to exercise those controls have to be shared with those who are responsible for costs, general financial data, such as profit, management reserves, contingency funds, and the like should not be shared with all the project staff.

Still, your business plan for the project, the game plan, has to contain sufficient data to show those who invest (whether upper management;

banks, or other investors) that the project will not only be successful, it will result in an acceptable return on any investment (ROI).Unless the ROI meets company or investor standards, the project is not worth the resources it commands.

If the government of the host country funds your project, the requirements for the job often precede the funding authorization by many months. Typical of such projects are all military programs, most communications projects, road or airport construction, and other infrastructure-enhancing work. When the effort begins, the money for these projects is not always defined or even earmarked as a line item in the annual budget. Although caution is required, in-country partners and representatives can help assure that funding is available in time to make the venture profitable.

The customer often hires consultants to do a "should-cost" estimate for a government-funded project, and sometimes for commercial projects as well. That estimate—invariably too low for any contractor to accept—will be the baseline against which all the bids are measured. Employees negotiating the project will not have authority to go above that figure unless all the bids exceed it. In that case, the project may be subject to cancellation. Often the customer will tell you the budget limitations. It is rare that the limit can be exceeded without a great deal of governmental action. By getting involved early in the project's evolution, a contractor can help make sure that many such funding issues are resolved before governmental funding decisions are made.

Purely commercial projects—building a factory or office facility, or upgrading a manufacturing capability—don't normally experience a funding problem because funding is approved along with the project.

The financial part of the game plan for any project will refer to the schedule, the selling price and the costs of the project, and any risks and opportunities that may affect project finances. It should include at least the following:

- Cost budget for each major functions of the project, based on the Work Breakdown Structure shown in Chapter 6.

- Costs associated with subcontractors.

- Expenditure rate, the time referenced rate at which dollar resources are consumed—sometimes referred to as "burn rate." It includes cash outflow as well as salary/wage obligations.

- Payment schedule, tracked against the expenditure rate, to show any points at which the project is scheduled to be cash negative and allow for calculations on the cost of money and any internal rates of return or interest earned.

- Payment guarantees on hand or needed, such as bonds and letters of credit.

- Discussion on exchange rates and currency stability: Even if the contract is paid in U.S. dollars, exchange rate changes affect the cost of the program to the customer, placing it at risk in the future.

- Description of how progress against the schedule and budget will be measured (the Certified Progress system described in Chapter 7).

The preliminary financial plan will have to be adjusted as the Integrated Master Plan (IMP) and the Integrated Master Schedule (IMS) are more fully detailed.

Many countries impose an obligation known as an "offset requirement" for larger, government-funded projects, though rarely for small projects of $10 million or less. The purpose of the requirement is to help offset the cost of the project, or the outflow of hard currency, by requiring the foreign contractor to make certain investments. These can range from the trivial, such as use of the national airline for travel to the country, to burdensome, such as an investment in the national infrastructure corresponding to the contract value. Often, the investment is in an unrelated business venture, which can create additional challenges for your company.

The manager of the international project is not directly concerned with the offset requirement, but it can become an issue for company management. The challenge is to avoid losing the profit of the project on the offset activity. Because the specific offset activity is usually selected by the contractor, once again, the in-country representative will play a key role. Properly done, an offset can generate additional profits for your company while satisfying the needs of the host government. Offsets are discussed in more detail in Chapter 10.

Negotiations for the project start with the very first contact anyone from your company makes with the customer's representative. They don't end until the project is completed and the final payment made. Working through the actual legal conditions of the contract is only one phase of the negotiation, but it is an important one.

As project manager, you must caution each person who deals in any way with the customer to keep in mind that the customer is always negotiating. If any conversation, no matter how insignificant it seems, touches on what the company will or will not do on the project—especially on payments, finances, or costs—that conversation must be referred to the project manager. Technical people like engineers who worked on my projects always told their counterparts, "I don't talk money or schedule."

Every position paper, "white" paper, and tradeoff analysis the company prepares for the customer will be filed and kept by the customer, as will notes on every conversation. Americans tend to be careless about this, but your customers will not be. Every communication will become backup for negotiations. It is to your negotiating advantage to be as diligent as your customer about keeping detailed records.

As a final note on getting to contract, the contract with your customer must specify the criteria for job completion. You and he both have to agree on what will confirm that the job is completed. I have seen too many projects lose money in the last weeks because the contract was not clear on the completion criteria.

Most of the projects I managed had a verification phase. I normally define the end of the project as the customer's signature on the test report. But whether or not your project has such a phase, you must define with the customer the point at which you have completed what you agreed to do. That point must be as objective as possible, not subject to opinion.

In today's international environment, payment terms are more important than ever. The world is hardly stable. Economic downturns, wars and threats of war, economic sanctions against certain countries and blocs of countries, and the potential of terrorist activities throughout the world all dictate the need to ensure the stability of payments to your company. The company needs favorable payment terms—and favorable means the sooner the better.

In an ideal world, the customer will pay in full at the beginning of the project. Although I've never seen such an ideal payment plan, contracts specifying 50 percent up front and reserving 10 percent as a performance bond are common. The other 40 percent would be paid at specified project milestones. If your customer country is not one of the "hard currency" countries, this would be a reasonable payment schedule.

If that kind of payment schedule is not acceptable to the customer, there are other ways to keep project cash positive. The most common are bonds, letters of credit, and the other bank instruments discussed in Chapter 3.

Several times I have mentioned the importance of an in-country presence. Without an effective in-country representative, it is unlikely that any international effort can be successful. Whether the in-country office is an individual or a large staff, it is the liaison between the project manager and the customer. It allows the customer to talk face-to-face with a person who represents the project manager and his company. The office at the same time can give the project manager a reliable analysis of the business environment in the country, the customer's opinions, and the local political situation, and can advise on how to make the project successful. I have never seen a successful project managed solely from stateside.

Among the functions of the in-country representative are to:

- Represent the company and project manager to the customer.

- Represent the customer to the project manager and the company.

- Help keep the project sold (given the time it often takes to get to contract, political pressures to cancel projects are common).

- Support the project with in-country assistance, such as hotel and car reservations, communications support, office space, interpreters, and secretarial help.

- Arrange meetings with the customer.

- Arrange meetings with U.S. government offices, such as consulates, attaches, and others.

- Help educate the customer on meeting the requirements of the U.S. government, especially concerning technical data transfers.

- Help project personnel with housing arrangements.

- Help find in-country support and subcontractors for the project.

- Keep the project management informed of the local economic and political situation.

These responsibilities are why selection of the in-country representative is important. He may be someone from your own company, from a local company, or even a contracted consultant. The person should not be selected based solely on the desire to reside in that country, though that will certainly be necessary.

The selection requires the same care and concern as hiring any other manager that is a direct report to the project manager. If he is to be effective and the customer is to have confidence in him, the customer must be aware of that relationship.

Some useful criteria for selecting an in-country representative, whether for a single project or for continuing representation of the company, are these:

- This may seem obvious, but I've seen it violated many times. The representative selected must be thoroughly trained in all aspects of the company; its officers, the products and services offered, and the managers and core staff of each project in work. This rule has regularly been violated on the rationale that the representative selected had valuable contacts in the host country. Though that may seem a sound reason, contacts are in fact not as important as knowledge of the company he is representing. On the other hand, he must also pass the following tests, or his technical expertise could be made moot by cultural or political blunders.

- The representative must realize that she has customers both in country and back home at the plant. She must be able to serve both, representing the company to the customer and the customer to the company.

- In large companies that have several projects in work in a given country, the representative must be able to work with all the projects and their managers and must understand the objectives, services, and products of each.

- In many countries, the representative must both speak the language and understand the customs. In some countries, the language is not as important as in others but comprehensive cultural knowledge, especially of business customs, is critical everywhere.

- Previous experience in the business and the country is valuable.

- There is no universal answer to the question of whether the representative should be of local nationality or from the United States, but all other factors being equal, a savvy, sensitive, and knowledgeable U.S. citizen is generally more successful than a local person, especially if he also speaks the language. The U.S. citizen also is perceived as having more authority than would a local citizen.

- While I have seen people remain effective as in-country representatives for as long as 30 years, most should be replaced after about five to seven years. Much of the representative's effectiveness derives from the quality of the relationship between company and customer. If there are periods of legal disagreements, such as arbitration, the effectiveness of the representative can be quite short-lived.

RECAPITULATION

The importance of a strong game plan cannot be overstated. It sets the stage for the entire project and establishes the structure for the IMP and IMS. The game plan helps both identify and mitigate many potential risks early. It helps the project manager to visualize the entire project from cradle to grave. The astute manager of an international project will spend considerable energy on drafting an effective game plan.

The purpose of the game plan is to analyze the project from beginning to the end to reduce risks and to anticipate and choreograph all the activities required to bring the project to a successful conclusion. The six basic elements of the game plan are:

1. Project description.

2. Marketing plan.

3. Description and analysis of the competition and the competitive environment.

4. Description of how the project will be performed.

5. List of key personnel and their roles.

6. Financial data.

Though the plan may have more sections, these are the basics that all plans should cover. Most problems on a project can be traced to lack of adequate planning in the early phases.

Gathering information on competitors can be risky if your customer is the U.S. government. A company can be deemed unqualified if its personnel violate the rules intended to maintain fairness.

How the manager conceives of the project as progressing and the list of key personnel are closely tied; together they demonstrate his vision of how to succeed with the project. If he changes his concept, the key personnel list should probably be modified to match the new concept.

The financial data are used for (1) presenting the case for the project to upper management and (2) setting the baselines for the financial control system for the project. (The financial control system is discussed in Chapter 7.)

Customer contact that could result in modifications to the work must be tightly controlled. The contract must specify who can direct and who can accept changes to the Statement of Work, and under what conditions and criteria.

The contract must also include exit criteria. It must be specific as to what constitutes completion of the project so as to avoid conflict at the end of the work.

In Part II of this book—*Defining the Project*—the management tools necessary to run the project are explained. Organizing and staffing the project, both in-plant and overseas, are covered in the next chapter.

PART II

DEFINING THE
PROJECT

CHAPTER 6

ORGANIZING AND STAFFING THE PROJECT

GETTING STARTED

As soon as your company decides to submit a proposal for a project, set up the Project Room—often called a proposal, war room, or meeting room. Access to the room should be restricted to the project team and management only. The room should be equipped with all the necessary reference materials anyone might need for any part of the project, plus any standards, external specifications, the Request for Proposal from the customer, the Instructions for Bidders (if there are any), a copy of the contract once it's completed, and all the other documents prepared in support of the project.

The project room needs work stations with computers, room for flip charts on easels, and wall space for proposal storyboard reviews (portable corkboard panels are often used). Gantt and PERT charts showing the proposal effort should be posted early, and progress of the program should be tracked visibly against the draft plan and the proposed schedule. Any metrics chosen for each section of the team should also be posted. Once the project gets underway, status briefings should be held in that room.

Organizing and staffing project, international or domestic, is approached in six basic steps, though we will talk later about additional considerations for international projects. The basic steps are:

- Prepare the Work Breakdown Structure (WBS).

- Prepare the Specification Tree and write the specifications.

- Write the Statement of Work (SOW).

- Draw up the Integrated Master Plan (IMP).

- Set up the Integrated Master Schedule (IMS).

- Identify needs and acquire the staff required for the project.

THE WORK BREAKDOWN STRUCTURE

The fact that international projects require overseas staff means that you must plan for additional support and enhance the selection criteria for those personnel. For a project within the United States, management doesn't have to worry much about different cultures (though a Californian might find the culture of South Carolina a bit odd—and vice versa); nor does it have to worry about housing and transportation beyond approving expense reports. Overseas, however, is a different matter. So for international projects, there are additional challenges:

- The culture of the host country and region has to be taken into account during the staffing phase.

- If the customer wants to participate as an active member of the project, responsibilities have to be allocated appropriately. There may need to be a "Purchaser's Responsibilities" section to the contract.
- The incentive plan for the in-country team has to be hammered out.

- Additional concerns will be:
  —The in-country office and its staff.
  —Housing for employees in-country.
  —Transportation for employees and any families.
  —Medical care.
  —Dependent education.
  —Difficulties of control.

Before the project can be staffed, it must be segmented in terms of the skills needed and the level of staffing for each identified skill. In the previous chapter, Figure 5.1 compared skill sets needed with available personnel to help in the staffing decision. But to what work element the skill sets are needed, the project must first be structured in a way that helps the manager identify the needs. This is accomplished through a work breakdown structure (WBS).

The WBS identifies in as fine detail as possible the particulars of the project and each of its elements. It can be organized by skills required for the project (systems engineering, software engineering, integrated logistics system, verification, etc.) or by the subsystems of the major system (primary structure subsystem, power subsystem, communications subsystem, etc.). Either method can be used for almost any project. The former has advantages in a company organized in the matrix style typical of the defense industry, allowing each element of the functional organization to identify and manage its piece of the whole system, though some form of responsibility assignment matrix may be needed to parse out organization elements to the products and services that might be distributed among the elements of the WBS elements.

A WBS based on deliverable project subsystems is the one demonstrated in this book because it is better for most other applications. It, too, has a potential weakness when the project requires preparation of a large number of specifications. For instance, preparing one software specification may be so preferable to preparing multiple software specifications that the WBS structure would favor the organizational over the subsystem breakdown method. Trade-offs must be made between the significant costs of preparing specifications and the efficiency of the WBS structure. Because commercial projects don't require the same level of specifications as government or defense projects, the issues will be more easily resolved.

Discussions on the relative advantages of each WBS philosophy have been held for years in every company involved in such projects. No advantage of one over the other clearly applies in all cases. The project manager usually has to decide which way to go. However, in many recent projects, the customer has dictated the WBS, taking the decision out of the manager's hands. This is almost always the case when the customer is a prime or second-tier contractor in a consortium because it is to the customer's advantage to have the subordinate contractor's WBS mesh with his own without the cross-reference documents that would otherwise be required. In that case, the project manager makes the necessary accommodations in her own organization.

To refresh your recollection, the log cabin example has seven major subsystems:

- Land preparation.

- Primary structure subsystem.

- Access subsystem.

- Power subsystem.

- Plumbing subsystem.

- Heating and air conditioning subsystem.

- Communications subsystem.

Each of these major subsystems will be further dissected into its elements, including the materials and labor required. Figure 6.1 is the top-level WBS for our example. To build the plan, the schedule, the financial control system, and the risk management system, the WBS will have to be elaborated in much more detail. The top-level chart is used to demonstrate the process to be used.

In Figure 6.1, the chart shows the project documentation effort, the seven major subsystems, and some of the lower-level elements of each of those subsystems.

Figure 6.2 shows the same WBS in a spreadsheet format that may be easier to manipulate as changes are made. As the WBS evolves, the manager is better able to visualize the work that must be performed to complete the project. He can also begin to identify the specific skills necessary for the job, and tentatively project the timing required for those skills, though that will not be totally clear until the IMP and the IMS come together. (See Appendix C for the complete WBS for the Europistania Log Cabin Project.)

FIGURE 6.1
EUROPISTANIA LOG CABIN PROJECT
Work Breakdown Structures

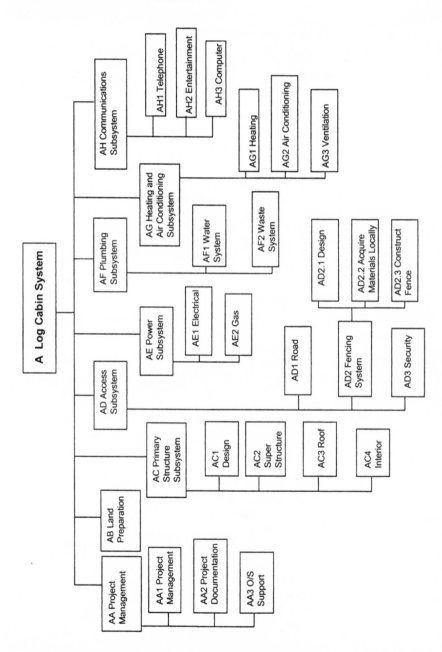

FIGURE 6.2
EUROPISTANIA LOG CABIN PROJECT

Work Breakdown Structure (Partial List)

A Log Cabin System
    AA Project Management
        AA1 Project Management Office (PMO)
            AA1.1 Project Manager
            AA1.2 Assist PM (Overseas)
            AA1.3 Project Controls
        AA2 Project Documentation
            AA2.1 Systems Specification
            AA2.2 Statement of Work
            AA2.3 Integrated Master Plan
            AA2.4 Integrated Master Schedule
            AA2.5 Export Licenses
            AA2.5.1 Review Doc List
            AA2.5.2 Prepare Documentation
            AA2.5.3 Submit to Dept of Commerce
            AA2.6 Technical Assistance Agreement
            AA2.6.1 Prepare Documentation
            M2.6.2 Submit for Customer's Approval
            AA2.6.3 Submit to US Dept of State
        AA3 Overseas Support
    AB Land Preparation
        AB1 Clearing
        AB2 Remove Debris
        AB3 Grading
        AB4 Trenching
    AC Primary Structure Subsystem
        AC1 Design and Architectural Drawings
        AC2 Superstructure
            AC2.1 Design
            AC2.2 Acquire materials for primary structure
            AC2.3 Ship materials
            AC2.4 Transport materials to site
            AC2.5 Lay foundation
            AC2.6 Construct superstructure
        AC3 Roof
            AC3.1 Design
            AC3.2 Acquire materials for roof (local purchase)
            AC3.3 Transport materials to site
            AC3.4 Construct roof
        AC4 Interior
            AC4.1 Design
            AC4.2 Acquire materials and furniture
            AC4.3 Ship materials
            AC4.4 Transport materials to site
            AC4.5 Construct interior
            AC4.6 Install furnishings

A common error of project managers is not putting enough detail in the WBS to make it useful in managing the project. All entries in the WBS are either tasks to be performed or a summary title for all tasks below that level. The first three levels are generally summary entries and the fourth and the lower levels are task entries, though there are exceptions to both. No task listed should require less than eight hours to perform. These are not staff-hours, but clock hours. Also, no task should take longer than 80 hours (two weeks) to be completed.

Assigning most tasks a duration of about 40 hours, with 80 as a maximum and eight as a minimum, the project manager should be able to maintain good insight as to task status and exercise tight control over progress of each element at the weekly project meetings. Longer tasks, such as those scheduled to take a month, become difficult to manage and report on—they tend to become miniprojects. Typically, at the beginning the supervisor will report that the task has started on time. The second and third week, the supervisor will report that it is on schedule to finish as projected. Then, just when it is scheduled for completion, the supervisor reports that the task is now behind schedule and will take another one or two more weeks. If the task is on or near the critical path, that delay will throw the master schedule off, possibly placing the project at risk.

Keeping task lengths short gives the project manager better visibility and more control. This is particularly important on overseas projects due to the higher costs of schedule delays, and the frequent unpredictability of the total situation.

The project manager can use the top-level WBS to select the core team, because it identifies the expert skills required to start the project. For instance, at the beginning she needs someone skilled in land description, drainage, aquifers, and the many other elements necessary for the proper clearing, grading, and preparation of the land for the cabin. She needs both a communications expert and personnel skilled in each of the major subsystems. This small crew of experts is the core team that will help organize and staff the project. Other skills that might be represented on the core team are project controls and scheduling (there will be discussion of these roles later).

The people selected for the core team may or may not eventually assume leadership roles for the project. An expert in a given discipline does not necessarily make a good subordinate manager. Decisions about management have to be made independently. In a matrix organization, however, the core team should be dedicated to the project and not have to juggle multiple projects.

The numbering system used for the WBS is a convenient way to identify the major element for each subordinate product. In the examples in Figures 6.1 and 6.2, the letter "A" refers to the log cabin project and will identify any work or subsystem associated with it. Usually, no other major project within the company would be designated with an "A."

The next digit, a letter A through H, identifies one of the major subsystems or a set of project-level tasks (licenses, SOW, systems specifications). The choice for this example is arbitrary. There may be personal or organizational preferences for selecting a different identification system. Product departmental designations might be used, for example. In this system of numbering, land preparation is identified as AB, the primary structure as AC, and so forth.

At the third and successive levels, it's common to use numerals, primarily because too many letters are easily confused. Each major subsystem is broken down into its primary elements and each of those is assigned a number. In this WBS, the roof of the structure is assigned AC4—A (Log Cabin Project), C (Primary Structure), 4 (Roof). Any work, any material, and any drawing or specification concerning the roof will carry AC4 as the first three digits of its own number. Subsequent numerals will be separated with periods, for example, AC4.5. You will sometimes see variations in this convention described, such as not using periods to separate the numerals, but the method we're using is usefully clear.

Each entry in the WBS represents a process or a set of tasks, each of which has inputs and outputs, and work performed. Each input must be an output of some other process and each output must be an input to another process, except, naturally, for the starting and ending entries (see Figure 6.3).

FIGURE 6.3
PROCESS INTERRELATIONS

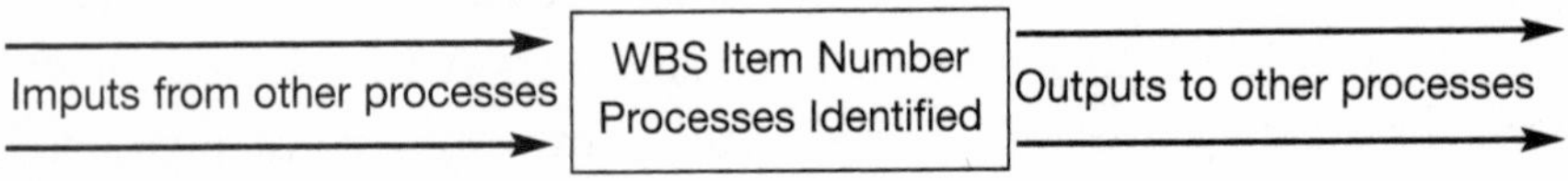

Imputs from other processes | WBS Item Number / Processes Identified | Outputs to other processes

As each process is identified and its needs (inputs) and products (outputs) become known, the information required to prepare the IMP and the IMS is building. I have used a few of the commercial software products on the market to help project planners with these efforts and found them quite adequate for the job.

Whether or not you use a software program, the procedure is the same:

- List each WBS item and the work process associated with it.

- Identify the information that will be needed before the process can begin.

- Identify where the information exists or the process that will produce the information.

At this point the chronological order of tasks begins to form. Figure 6.4 is an example that uses a few the WBS activities to demonstrate the process:

FIGURE 6.4
PROCESS ANALYSIS EXAMPLE

Inputs	*WBS Item or Process*	*Outputs*
Access granted Land survey results	AB Clear the land	Land clear with debris.
Truck contract	AB2 Remove debris	Staked and ready for grading.
Grading contract Grading stakes in place	AB3 Grade land	Land readied for construction of building and trenches.
Survey, infrastructure plans, electrical and sewage plans	AB4 Trenching	Readied to lay cables, water, and sewer lines.
Specifications, Customer input	AC1 Design and architectural drawings	Architectural drawings.
Architectural drawings, specifications	AC2.1 Design of superstructure	Bill of materials.
Bill of materials Vendor tradeoffs	AC2.2 Acquire materials	Materials ready to ship.
Contract transport Bill of materials	AC2.3 Ship materials	Materials arrive in port.
Materials on hand at port Trucking contract	AC2.4 Transport materials to site	Materials on hand at site.

Figure 6.4 represents only a small slice of the activity required to organize the WBS in a task order for preparing the IMS. In the early stages, there will be some blanks that will have to be analyzed, typically work products that have no output, or outputs that have no destination or purpose, as well as inputs or needs that have no source.

If a process has no output product, it has no purpose and should be eliminated from the WBS. If another process requires an input that isn't included as an output from another process or task, another task must be added that produces the needed product. Other processes as well as more details of the project are exposed through this analysis. Organizing the WBS is an iterative process that requires the active participation of the entire core team. The analysis takes a commitment of time that may seem excessive, but the planning phase is critical. Time spent here will save you the much higher costs that would otherwise occur later. An old saying in project management is that "There's never enough time to do it right, but there's always enough time to do it over." Take the time you need up front to do it right.

SPECIFICATIONS

Since it is common to designate specifications developed during the project as deliverables to the customer, let's talk briefly about specifications. On a project on the scale of the example used, though the specifications would not normally be a deliverable, the architectural drawings likely would be. Those drawings are actually specifications in a different format.

Using the government's military standards as a very general guideline, larger projects require three levels of specifications. The "A" level is the Systems Specifications. These describe the entire system, its purpose, and its complete dimensions, among other specifics. In the systems spec, the interfaces among subsystems are described as well as any limits that might be imposed. Some interface's may require separate interface specs. The Systems Specifications document is the source of requirements for all subordinate specifications.

The next level of specification, the "B" level, deals with subsystem specifications. It details the specifics of the particular subsystem. It will also describe the interfaces of the components that make up the subsystem, including any hardware and software.

The "C" level specifications are the component specs for each subsystem element, as well as any detailed interface specifications that might be required, such as in the communications subsystem.

On large military projects or on government projects having large software components, the B and C level specifications will be further divided into B1 through B5 specifications, and C1 through C5 specifications. In this case, your company will have to refer to the documents listed in the RFP and the Information for Bidders (IFB).

Each specification requires basic information. It may be voluminous for major projects or only a few pages for smaller projects or components of larger projects. The first draft of a large military satellite program I worked on was a single sheet of paper on which the concept was described. Later, the specifications filled several bookcases.

While it is certainly not necessary to use the military standard system, its guidelines are a handy way to organize specifications on a project. At the least, you will in any case need some way to identify the drawings and specifications of the system and subsystems of the project. Figure 6.5 depicts a specification tree for our project.

FIGURE 6.5
SPECIFICATION TREE FOR THE EUROPISTANIA LOG CABIN PROJECT

A-Level	B-Level	C-Level
Europistania logable plans systems specs.	Land subsystem specification	Survey drawings. Water wells specifications.
	Primary structure subsystem specification	Architectural drawings. Materials specifications. Load-bearing wall specifications.
	Access subsystem specification	Road drawings and specifications. Security subsystem specifications. Fence specifications.
	Power subsystem specification	Electrical power subsystem specifications. Gas subsystem specifications.
	Backup power specifications. Plumbing subsystem specification	Water subsystem specifications. Waste subsystem specifications.
	Heating and air conditioning subsystem specification	Heating specifications. Air conditioning specifications. Ventilation specifications.
	Communications subsystem specification	Telephone network specifications. Entertainment specifications. Computer and Internet interface specifications.

Regardless of its level, each specification document should have the following main sections:

- *Introduction, purpose, and overview.* This section will give an overview of the system being described and the boundaries of the specification, i.e., what it includes and what, if anything, it does not include. It will state the purpose of the specification and often the reasons the customer needs the project.

- *References.* All references used as resources in drawing up the specifications should be cited. Among these might be any U.S. government requirements; technical standards; any applicable company directives, standards, and procedures; and customer-imposed documentation. These last typically include International Standards Organization (ISO) and other international standards.

- *Technical Requirements.* This section sets out all the firm requirements of the system, subsystem, or component being specified and any other criteria the customer might want on record.

- *Logistics.* Any repair parts, manuals, maintenance, training, or other services and documentation needed will be described here.

- *Glossary of Terms.* Abbreviations and terms not part of the common vocabulary should be explained.

- *Cross References.* If needed, a cross-reference guide to other specifications or documents could be included.

Within the technical section a convenient convention is used to identify the "firm" or "hard" requirements that must be satisfied in order to complete the project successfully. The convention states that requirements using the verb "shall" are firm, and those using "will" are non-firm. For instance, a possible systems specifications requirement sentence might be: "The exterior walls of the log cabin *shall* be of Ponderosa Pine logs, which *shall* be a minimum of 12 inches in diameter (+1 inch, -1/2 inch) and maximum of 14 inches (+ 1/2 inch, - 1 inch) and diameter *will* not vary more than 1 inch over the length." It contains two requirements that must be met, and one the customer desires but does not require.

Any "shall" requirement must be verifiable. It must specify how it can be confirmed that the requirement has been met—test, demonstration, analysis, inspection—or it is not a legitimate requirement. In the example, the contractor could be found non-compliant if either the type of log used in the construction of the cabin or the diameter of any of the logs exceeds the limits of the specification. It could not be found in violation for minor variations in the diameter over the length of the log that exceeded the desired 1 inch. Meeting non-firm requirements is important to enhance customer satisfaction with the final product.

As for the WBS, specifications at each level may have to be modified or changed as more knowledge is gained. The top-level specification, the systems spec, is normally part of the contract and the customer must approve any change. Requirements for subordinate specifications will be changed to conform when the systems specification is modified. These are easily traced, because subordinate specifications derive their requirements from the systems specification in the first place.

Because all system specifications requirements must flow down to lower-level specifications, a requirement stated in the systems specification might be included in more than one subordinate specification. Each hard requirement must be able to be tracked so that a change in one subordinate specification can be traced first to the original systems specification requirement and further to other subordinate specification documents that contain the same or a derived requirement. For instance, a modification to the wall of our log cabin may also require a change to the roof or a window, or to the power or communications subsystems. The ability to track is also is needed for later testing or verification. The sooner the project manager understands the total impact of any change the better he can manage the changes and estimate the cost.

This knowledge also helps when decisions must be made about whether the costs of consequential changes, say, can be added to the stand-alone costs of changing the wall design. All projects must have a means of making the changes requested by the customer or recommended by the contractor and costing them out so that a price can be given to the customer in the form of a change proposal.

Even if a recommended change actually brings about an ultimate reduction in project costs, there are costs associated with making the change that will at least reduce the magnitude of the reduction. Drawings and specifications have to be changed, verifications and tests have to be modified, schedules are affected, and new materials must be programmed into the system—all of which require work by the project team. There is rarely a truly cost-free change to a project. The total costs associated with the change have to be compared to the benefits gained from the change. Whether or not you charge the customer for the change, the project will bear a cost.

THE STATEMENT OF WORK

For the project team, the statement of work (SOW) is the most useful document. The SOW describes the specific tasks required of each section of the project team, translating the language of the contract and systems specification into the common language used by project team members. The SOW applies to subcontractors as well as members of the company. Work by subcontractors that is required will all be included in the main document and a separate SOW will have to be prepared for each subcontractor. The SOW carries the same force as the contract, and is usually second in the list of priorities. In case of discrepancy, the contract has top priority, the SOW second, and the system specifications third.

The convention related to use of *shall* and *will* also applies to the SOW. Each use of the verb *shall* should be referenced to a specification document or the contract using the unique identification number of the requirement. The SOW may have any number of derived requirements that are not specifically stated in the specifications or contract but are required to meet the specifications. It should not, however, initiate any new requirement unrelated to the basic specifications.

SOW requirements have to be identified with the source requirement because at the end of the project the verification process will use them to prove that the project has completed all the requirements.

The project manager must be alert to the tendency to enhance requirements. Often as later documents are prepared, there is "requirements creep." As a requirement is stated in more detail in each document, it becomes enhanced beyond the contract—and beyond what was incorporated into the price. Requirement enhancing can be identified during design reviews, but the project manager must be alert to it. The customer is often similarly to blame for requirements creep.

Another common cause of requirements creep is the frequent replacement of managers. Each subsequent manager tends to yield points to the customer, some of which turn out to be highly expensive for the project.

The three types of specifications documents are normally deliverables to the customer. Though the specifications are not universally deliverable, I mention them because on large programs they are often on the list of deliverables. The documents discussed next are not normally on the list of deliverables but they may be. Whether or not they are, though, they are important to the project manager and to upper management of the company.

THE INTEGRATED MASTER PLAN

The IMP, as I have mentioned, is the document that explains how the project will be performed, the responsibilities of team members, and how the subcontractors, both domestic and international, fit into the overall project. The IMP is not the same as the IMS, though project managers often make the error of calling the schedule the plan. It is not.

The IMP is the project manager's documented vision for the conduct of the project. It states any exceptions and modifications to the company's standard processes that may be required for the project, explains how any ambiguous elements will be interpreted, and describes how customer expectations will be met. It sets out the general chronological order of activities, identifies tasks that must be completed before the project even moves overseas, and states how progress will be verified. It should define milestone events and the criteria for demonstrating that those events have occurred. If they are not included elsewhere, the IMP should also include an organization chart and a responsibility assignment matrix spelling out the specific responsibilities of each element of the organization and the level of authority for each subordinate manager.

Often the IMP is expressed visually in a PERT chart showing the order of tasks and the interrelationships among them. The PERT chart shown in

Project Management (AA) (a complete PERT chart is not included due to its size), and depicts project documentation, the export license process, and the Technical Assistance Agreement process. The number below the box is the number of working days assigned to the process, and the number above it is for the number of people working on the process over that duration. As the chart evolves, other information will be added, such as most optimistic, most pessimistic, and most likely durations; resources; critical paths; and other information of interest to the project manager.

FIGURE 6.6
PERT CHART SAMPLE OF WBS AA

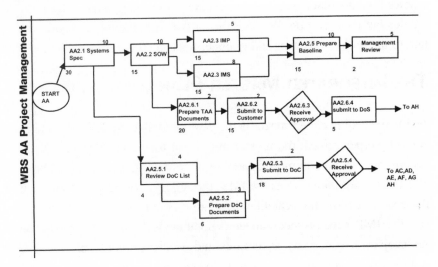

Task relationships can be made more detailed by identifying them as:

- *Finish-to-Start (FS)* is the normal relationship between tasks, indicating that one task must finish before the next chronological task starts.

- *Finish-to-Finish (FF)* indicates that the two tasks must finish at the same time, or the first cannot be considered complete until the second completes. This may be used when the outputs of the two tasks are required in order for a third to begin.

- *Start-to-Start (SS)* indicates that the two tasks may begin simultaneously. In this case the two tasks may either be Start tasks, or that they both use the same output of a previous process.

The better the relationships are defined, the more meaningful is the chart and the more useful in planning work-around activities and other risk mitigation efforts.

THE INTEGRATED MASTER SCHEDULE

The IMS shows the start dates and durations of each major activity of the project, as well as the subordinate details. It is a handy vehicle for showing upper management the progress (or lack thereof) of the project. The schedule is usually shown in Gantt chart format. It can include the relationships among the tasks as well as any more complex criteria.

The schedule is derived from the contract requirements. The customer will require that the project be completed a stated number of months after the beginning of the work or award of the contract. Though that period will have been negotiated, it will generally present a challenge to the contractor in terms of time and human resources. A typical contract specifies a penalty for exceeding the contract period by more than a defined number of days. It should also have an incentive for performing better than required, "bringing it in under schedule."

Under ideal circumstances, the schedule could be built bottom-up, with each subordinate element deriving its own schedule and then integrated into the IMS. Although this attracts 100 percent buy-in by subordinate managers, it invariably results in a schedule that is unacceptably long to both the customer and the project manager.

Early in negotiation of the project, perhaps even in the IFB and the RFP, the customer will express requirements for the period of performance. Accordingly, early in the project the project manager will state a top-down performance period requirement into which the subordinate elements must fit their schedules. The project manager's requirement should be shorter than the customer's by at least 10 percent to build some slack time into the schedule. If there is an incentive for completing the project on a shorter schedule is included, the shorter schedule should be the basis on which the project manager reserves the designated percent of slack.

There are certain tasks specifically associated with an international project that have to be included in the schedule. For one thing, if there are items being exported that are considered a transfer of technology or that can be considered to be in the category of international trade in arms, both require licenses from the Department of State and signatures from the end-user as well as the companies involved and officials from the U.S. government. Getting the licenses and signatures can easily take six months. Approval cycles for Department of Commerce export licenses are not so long but must also be considered.

Shipping time—from preparation for shipping, packaging, and transport to port through actual transportation time, receiving in country, customs, and transport to site—will often exceed 30 days, but it can be scheduled because companies that handle overseas shipments can predict with reasonable accuracy the total time required for the goods to arrive in port, whether by sea or air, and will advise you when the goods must be ready to ship. Keep in mind, though, that missing a shipping date may mean not just a day-for-day slippage but possibly a week-for-day slippage because transport to the country where you need the goods may not be frequent.

Clearance of customs in the receiving country, however, is often unpredictable. Goods may be delayed for any number of political or administrative reasons. The in-country partner or representative must be familiar with customs procedures and help clear the goods at that end. Often the customer can assist. It is common for the customer to pay the customs fees.

The major constraints to schedules for any international project, then, are start and end dates, license processing, transport overseas, and customs. All other tasks have to be scheduled with those restrictions in mind.

Shown in Figure 6.7 is a partial Gantt chart (for the complete chart, see Appendix A) of the Log Cabin Project, showing the Project Management Office (PMO) and Land Preparation portions of the project. In this early stage, we don't know how long the project will take so initially we show it as a 12-month project. As planning progresses and the necessary links and predecessor activities are better defined, the actual duration of the project will become more clear.

This is an excellent chart for demonstrating the current status of the project for briefings and reviews. The software program can generate a "time now" line, and the current completion status can be added along each task line to show actual progress. However, though excellent for presentation purposes and for display in the Project Room, it is not adequate for the project manager's control of the project. He needs much more (see Chapter 7).

FIGURE 6.7
GANTT CHART SAMPLE OF THE LOG CABIN PROJECT (WBS AA AND AB)

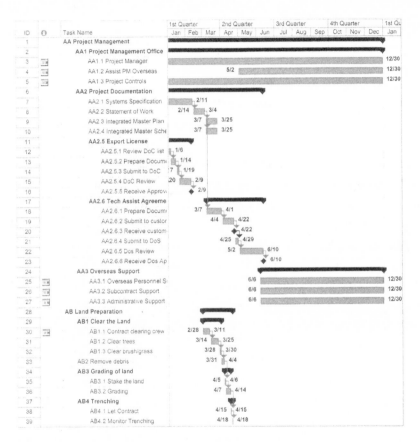

The IMS will cover all tasks to the lowest level. It should be posted on the wall in the Project Room for all team members to review regularly. Schedule status should be reported at least weekly for large programs, daily for smaller programs.

The elements included in the schedules presented to various levels of management within and above the project are the WBS items to as low a level as the particular manager requires visibility. Each manager has unique needs for information, but generally two levels down is sufficient detail for most.

The PERT chart for the IMP and the Gantt chart for the IMS are derived from the same basic data but show the project differently. The Gantt chart displays the on-time status of the project clearly. The PERT chart provides a means to analyze discrepancies and design work-around approaches in case of schedule slippage. Both are valuable for the project manager.

GETTING ORGANIZED

There are basically two ways to organize the project. The first is to organize around an established, well-working team. The second is to organize by project task. Either will work—or fail—depending on the specifics of the project and the company, and both apply equally to domestic and to international business.

A project must have both a well-organized, efficiently functioning team and a task-oriented organization. The old argument about whether projects should be project-organized or functionally managed by a matrix organization is never-ending. There is no single solution. A project typically requires both.

The basic weaknesses of each method of organizing a project are clear. A purely project-oriented organization doesn't take advantage of the wider range of skills that might be available throughout the company. A purely functionally managed project isn't sufficiently focused on a single set of project priorities.

Look at the skills needed to perform each task and choose the best available candidate for it. Usually, the project manager will choose people he knows he can depend on, people he has worked with before. However, there are likely be some new skills needed that will require fresh talent.

With all the tasks of the WBS identified, the next step is to assign resources to those tasks, whether these are monetary, personnel, or both. This effort may affect the original PERT chart because some key personnel may be required for more than one task but can only work on one at a time. A Work Package Planning Sheet (sometimes called a Task Planning Sheet), which will be discussed in the next chapter, will help match resources to tasks.

The normal company selection processes can be used for work performed at the company plant. Such work might be design, preparation of specifications, writing the SOW, and other similar tasks, but it might also include complete construction of one or more subsystems, such as a unique complex communications system, to prove they work. With a one-of-a-kind design, it is better to build and test it in the plant, where there are experts and facilities available for support if there are problems. Solving problems that show up the first time overseas can be expensive.

For work performed in-country, there are additional considerations. For example, do not include on the in-country team anyone who will be irritated or offended by the customs of the country. Even off-the-cuff comments or jokes can be a strong indication of someone's discomfort with the culture. Such potential irritations can grow into serious problems after a few weeks on the job.

The customer may want to participate as an active member of the project. It may be that a portion of the project is set aside for the customer to perform, or it may be that her personnel become an integral part of the in-country, or even the in-plant, team.

> In one project in Italy, my customer wanted to provide a number of engineers to work with our engineers. We agreed to that, with the stipulation that one Italian engineer was equivalent to two-thirds of one of our engineers because of the language differences and their lack of familiarity with our processes. As it happened they made up for those shortcomings quite rapidly and carried their own weight—but we did not, of course, refund any money.

The schedule and costs of a project will be negatively impacted if there is high turnover of personnel on the overseas team. Because members of such a team are difficult to replace at all, and almost impossible to replace quickly, some sort of incentive package should be offered to those who hold on for the duration of the assignment, perhaps a bonus of a certain percentage of their salary, in addition to any pay differential offered for overseas assignment.

Housing for the in-country team must be arranged. It might be residence hotels or leasing of blocks of apartments to rotate personnel through as they come and go with specific skills. The number of in-country sites will also affect how the housing is handled, as well as whether family members are welcomed.

Transportation needs, both in support of the project and in support of the personal needs of employees, must be considered. Again, the number of sites, their remoteness, and whether families are included will affect the approach taken.

If families are part of the package, medical care and education for dependents must be considered.

All these considerations have associated costs that must be dealt with early in the negotiations.

Finally, the fact that exercising control over an in-country team can be difficult must be recognized in planning for who will be assigned to the project. This argues for choosing people who will carry out the policies and instructions of the project manager without requiring an undue amount of supervision. In my discussions with other international project managers, we all have had the common experience of some team members becoming helpless when they arrived in country. They expected the company to solve all their personal problems and pay for extras like newspapers, personal trips in taxis, and even daily snacks. Clearly, people with such an attitude need to be culled from the list as early as possible.

WHAT WE DECIDED

For the Europistania Log Cabin Project, the WBS (Appendix C) and the full Gantt chart (Appendix A) have been completed, but though the tasks are largely defined, there are still a few that are more than two weeks in duration, so there is scrubbing to do on those tasks to break them down into subtasks.

We decide to send only supervisory personnel overseas and to hire the project work force from local companies. This plan has some risks, but our own visits in country and discussions with the customer make it seem feasible. Though we like the idea of using specifications, we have elected not to follow the military standard system completely. Instead, we will prepare shorter specifications tied to the technical requirements. We will prepare detailed SOWs for both our own employees and our subcontractors.

We will use management software (Microsoft Project®, Primavera®, or some other software program) to generate the necessary charts from the input data.

RECAPITULATION

Organizing a project starts with organizing the Project Room, where all the documents associated with the program are stored and some are displayed. It will be equipped with workstations and tables so the team can work together as needed in a focused environment.

There are six steps in organizing and staffing project:

1. Prepare the WBS.

2. Prepare the Specification Tree and write the specifications.

3. Write the SOW.

4. Develop the IMP.

5. Develop the IMS.

6. Identify and acquire the skills necessary for staffing the project.

Organizing and staffing an international project must take into account:

• Local culture.

• Customer participation.

• Incentive plan.

• In-country housekeeping and administrative tasks.

• Difficulties of control.

The WBS can be organization-based, product-based, or customer-directed, but in any case it must be in sufficient detail to assist in management of the project. Tasks should be no less than eight hours long, nor longer than 80 hours.

The specifications must be organized so that interdependencies are easily recognized. The military standard for specifications is a good guide, though for commercial projects it should be only a general guide. Any specification should have these six sections:

1. Introduction, purpose, and overview.

2. References.

3. Technical requirements.

4. Logistics.

5. Glossary of terms.

6. Cross references.

The IMP is the mature version of the game plan. It is visually represented by a PERT chart.

The IMS is represented by a Gantt chart. The two charts, based on the same database, are different representations of the same information.

For personnel stationed in country, the project manager must take into account a number of considerations that do not apply to domestic projects. Among these are:

• Housing.

• Medical.

• Schooling for dependents.

• Transportation.

In the next chapter, a financial control system is introduced that gives the project manager the necessary means for controlling project costs and schedule. It also gives early warning of problems.

Between that system and the risk management program discussed in Chapter 8, the project manager will have the tools necessary to avoid the negative impacts of unforeseen events.

Chapter 7

Financial Controls as a Management Tool

Any business, project, or organization must have controls. There must be a method of making sure the company is headed where the leaders want it to go.

Any control system has at least four basic elements:

1. A means of measuring whatever parameter is being used.

2. A means of evaluating the significance of any variation in the parameters of interest.

3. A means of altering behavior if the need is indicated.

4. A communication system to transmit this information where it is needed.

The project manager and company management team need a control system because they are interested in the answers to three questions:

1. Will the project be completed on time?

2. Will the completed work meet the customer's expectations?

3. Will the project stay within budgeted costs?

If at any time during the project the answer to any of these questions is no, the managers will want to know the reasons and what can be done to correct the situation.

To complicate matters, the three questions are not independent of each other. As engineers often say to management, "Fast, cheap, and good—choose any two." There will always be trade-offs among time, quality, and costs.

The most powerful tool of the project manager is the financial control system. Even the U.S. government looks closely at the financial control systems in place when it reviews failed programs. Invariably, it finds that there were warning signs within the system that were either not recognized by the system administrators or ignored by the project manager.

UNDERSTANDING FINANCIAL CONTROLS

The subject of financial controls is broad. It includes initial calculations of the internal return on investment of the project to determine its worth to the company, international banking issues like letters of credit, performance bonds, and monetary exchange rates. These are discussed elsewhere in this book. Within the broad subject are those we discuss here—the ratios used to establish or to compare performance against various benchmarks, such as return on net assets (RONA), sales per employee, and many others.

The discipline underlying financial controls is referred to as criterion-based management. It is usually implemented through methods commonly called earned value systems. The management control system offered here is a modification of one that has been used for over 30 years by the U.S. government.

Though it is called a financial control system, it is really a *management* tool the project manager uses to control the *project*, not just the finances of the project. True, measurements are often expressed in terms of dollars and the terminologies use the word cost but only because these are convenient and easily understood vehicles for expressing the progress, or lack thereof, of the project. Certainly, the project manager should not make the common error of turning the system over to the company finance department.

There is a fallacy that says management control systems only work with large, complex projects. (The risk management system described in the next chapter often suffers from the same fallacy.) In fact, whether the project is large or small, it requires some control mechanism to maintain the budget and the schedule. Only the complexity of the tracking and reporting system and the level of detail needed vary with the size of the project.

Many terms used within the system can misdirect the project manager into believing that financial types would be the primary users of the system; *terms like budgeted cost, contract budget baseline, cost account manager, or actual costs*. Even calling it an earned value system, rather than the more appropriate *certified progress* system, supports that potential mistake.

The financial control system is so important to the ultimate success of the project, and so powerful a management tool, that only the project manager should be responsible for directing its implementation and evaluating its reports. I have had to replace finance supervisors who failed to grasp this important concept.

The finance department normally owns the software, the report-generating tools, and the process that administers the system. Finance has the skills needed to help the project manager interpret the results. However, the project manager who delegates—or abdicates—his responsibilities to manage the project will quickly find himself in charge of a troubled project.

The financial control, earned value, or certified progress system is implemented in the execution phase of the project. The plan, the WBS, the schedule, the budget, and the Work Package Planning Sheets all must be already approved by the project manager. Only then can a baseline can be established for the budget and the schedule. Once fixed, the baseline cannot afterward be changed without modifying the contract. It will become the standard against which to measure progress. In fact, most project management software programs have the same rule—once the baseline is established, it is fixed. Otherwise, it would hardly be a baseline. The only exception is a contractually initiated modification.

The integrity of the financial control system depends on the accuracy of the data it contains. Measuring labor requires times cards with accurate reporting of time expended against the WBS item, or the work package, as well as accurate recording of time-related expenses charged against material and other direct charges (ODC), such as travel expenses.

Control system integrity also depends on the precision of the work in process (WIP) estimates. The shorter the duration of each work package, the more precise will be the estimate.

APPLYING FINANCIAL CONTROLS

Some of the acronyms used in financial control systems are shown in Table 7.1.

TABLE 7.1
TYPICAL FINANCIAL CONTROL TERMS

ACWP   **Actual cost of work performed.** The actual costs are derived from labor rates and time card reports.

BAC   **Budget at completion.** This baseline budget does not include the management reserve (MR). It is the contract baseline budget less management reserve.

BCWP   **Budgeted cost of work performed.** This is the product of the WIP estimate and the total budget for the work package. When summed, it represents the total of all the work packages.

BOWS   **Budgeted cost of work scheduled.** This is the product of the WIP scheduled and the total budget for the work package. When summed, it represents the total of all the work packages scheduled.

CBB   **Contract budget baseline.** This is the contracted total cost amount, or the price less profit. Some companies have additional overhead categories to be considered.

CPI   **Cost performance index.** The CPI is the quotient produced by dividing the BCWP by the ACWR A CPI greater than 1.0 is favorable. Less than 1.0 is unfavorable.

EAC   **Estimate at completion.** This is the cost of the total project based on the current CPI and SPI.

LRE   **Latest revised estimate.** This figures results from a complete review and possibly a re-plan of the program from the current point to get a new estimate of costs to complete the project.

MR   **Management reserve.** This item is under the control of the project manager, though upper management often insists on its approval prior to any commitment of funds from it.

SPI   **Schedule performance index.** The SPI, an indicator of schedule performance, is calculated by dividing the BCWP by the BOWS. An SPI greater than 1.0 I favorable. Less than 1.0 is unfavorable.

TCPI   **To complete performance index.** Often misunderstood, TCPI is an indication of the performance the project team must comply with to meet the cost goals of the project.

WIP   **Work in process.** WIP is a measure of the work performed to date as it relates to specific WBS item work packages.

WPPS   **Work package planning sheet.** The detailed plan for a specific work package, including when it will start, its scheduled completion date, and how to measure the WIP for the item.

The terms used in the management control system are visually related as shown in Figure 7.1.

FIGURE 7.1
VISUAL REFERENCE FOR TERMINOLOGY

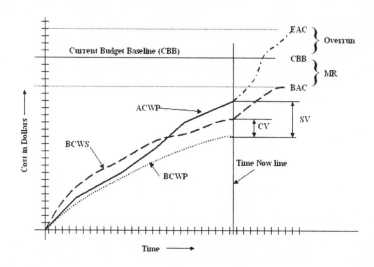

From the figure you can see how the schedule can be measured in dollars instead of time, which is convenient for showing the relationship between cost and schedule. It also clearly demonstrates how a schedule slip can affect the potential cost to correct a problem.

Figure 7.2 demonstrates the relationship among the various budget allocations in terms of what is of interest to upper management, what is under the control of the project manager with senior management approval, what the project manager can disburse with complete discretion, and what is allocated to various disciplines (the cost account managers).

The contract price contains the project cost baseline and profit. Company management is concerned with maintaining the profit and will exercise authority over the MR to protect that profit. The project manager is responsible for maintaining the contract budget baseline. She does so by withholding a portion of the budget allocated for this purpose until it is required for the work.

In a matrix organization, the project manager is under pressure to allocate the entire CBB to the control of the functional area managers, but if he does so, he abdicates his own responsibilities. He must resist that pressure and insist on retaining control over the budget allocations.

FIGURE 7.2
RELATIONSHIP OF BUDGET ALLOCATIONS

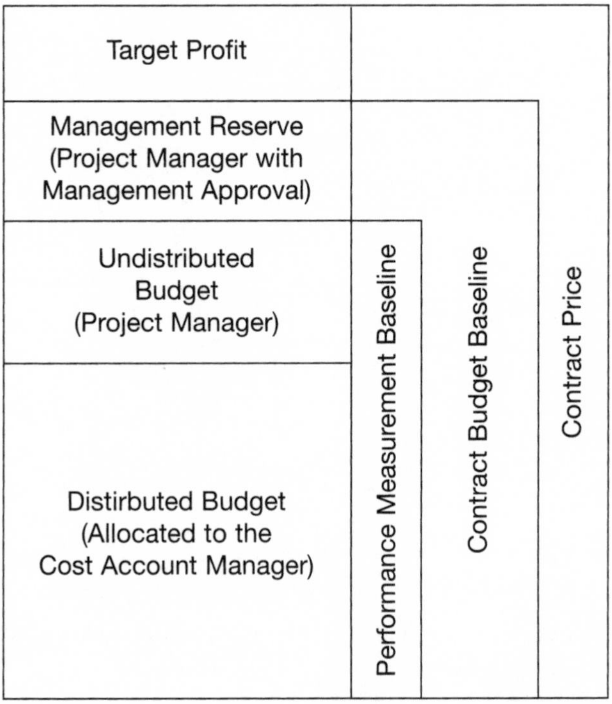

Cost account manager (CAM) is another unfortunate term in common usage for these management control systems that can lead the project manager to believe that the system is primarily financial. The CAM's are not financial department employees, they are subordinate managers within the project organization. They are responsible for ensuring that specified work is performed on time and within the budget allocated—the normal role of a manager. Their CAM responsibility is incidental. It simply refers to their responsibilities for measuring and reporting performance.

There are several means of measuring WIP, but if the work packages are of long duration, any measurement becomes difficult at best and imprecise at worst. Milestones must be established in advance with an appropriate percentage of completion assigned to each milestone, *without regard to the amount of labor expended against each milestone.*

Keeping work package durations to one or two weeks, as we discussed in the last chapter, allows the project manager or CAM to assign 50 percent complete when the task begins and the other 50 percent (equals 100 percent complete) when it ends. When there is a significant number of tasks, with weekly reporting, this can give a precise representation of the status of the project. It is the preferred metric for labor-intensive tasks.

In a production environment, units completed, expressed as a percentage of the total number to be completed, can be an accurate measure of value earned—a certification of progress.

The most inaccurate measure is level of effort (LOE). It can be used only with management work. Credit is given as labor is expended. This measure should never be used with more than 12 percent of the project WIP and only the project manager and a few selected members of the staff should use it.

The WIP measure for materials and other direct costs should be based on actual (invoice) costs compared against budgeted costs.

WPPS are used to spell out the details of specific tasks defined by the WBS. Among the information required are:

• A narrative description of the task.

• A scheduled breakdown of the task spread against the calendar, its milestones, and its budgeted costs by time period (weekly or monthly).

• The WIP measurement criteria, such as 0-100 percent (used for very short tasks), 50/50 percent, unit consumption, or LOE. If the tasks are broken down into one or two-week segments with milestones to indicate completion of each segment, the 50/50 percent WIP measurement will provide accurate data for the control system.

• The personnel or organizational resources assigned to do the work.

• A scheduled breakdown of budgeted material and ODC expenditures.

The CAM monitors progress against the WPPS, reporting it to the person responsible for administering project controls.

As the project moves along, a number of reports can be used to certify progress against the budget and schedule baselines. From these reports, the project manager will track the indexes that will give him early warning of a potentially adverse situation. The indexes and other reports help the project manager foresee problem areas and take appropriate measures, assuming he is knowledgeable of how the system works.

The formulas used to calculate the items used in this financial control system are:

- Schedule variance (SV) = BCWP - BCWS = $.
  As a percent, SV = (BCWP - BCWS)/BCWS = %.

- Cost variance (CV) = BCWP - ACWP = $.
  As a percent, CV = (BCWP - ACWP)/BCWP = %.

- At-completion variance = BAC - LRE.

- Schedule correlation (months behind schedule) = SV/Avg BCWP.

- Cost performance index (CPI) = BCWP/ACWP.

- Schedule performance index (SPI) = BCWP/BCWS.

- To-complete performance index (TCPI) = (BAC - BCWP)/(LRE - ACWP).

Estimates at completion:

- EAC1 = BAC/CPI.

- EAC2 = BAC/SPI.

- EAC3 = ACWP + (1/CPI) x (BAC - BCWP).

(These estimates should not be used in lieu of formal LRE preparations.)

The program controls software selected for the project will normally be able to calculate these common terms, or at least provide values for calculating the variables.

Any variance in cost or schedule requires investigation. Variances that exceed preset thresholds must require full reports to the project manager. Each report will explain the cause of the variance and its impact, as well as the corrective action planned to bring the parameter back into tolerance. Typically, thresholds are set at +/-5 percent and = >/= $K, where K represents 5 percent of the remaining budget for the measured WBS item. Positive as well as negative variances require investigation. Depending on the preferences of the project manager, these reports can be written or oral, but a written history of variances can prove valuable in detecting an emerging adverse trend.

Variances are reported not only for the project level but also for each subordinate manager that has CAM responsibilities. They are reported by period as well as by cumulative-to-date values. The latter threshold will normally be more restrictive than the periodic variance threshold.

Note that early variance reports may not accurately reflect the project's future. Typically, because projects have a difficult time with staffing in the early phases, the schedule is adversely affected and the costs favorably. Both are inaccurate indications of the true situation. After a few weeks, and certainly after staffing is completed, the situation will be self-correcting.

Cost and schedule variances and any adverse trends may indicate items to be reviewed by the Risk Management Board (see Chapter 8).

Variances may be caused by any number of situations. For instance:

- *Timing differences in the reports.* These variances are self-correcting over time.

- *Incorrect planning.* In this case, re-plan as early as possible to avoid an adverse impact on the entire project.

- *Uncontrolled work or expenses.* The CAM or the project manager must take hold of the reins with corrective action.

- *Changes in labor rates.* This is often a problem for large companies, especially in the defense industry. Since this is an external factor, there is little the project manager can do directly but he must manage so as to improve productivity (performance).

- *Labor force attrition.*

- *Fluctuations in materials prices.*

- *Variances in minimum-buy quantities.*

- *Changing scope of work.* This often happens, because of either bad planning or unstable leadership. Each new leader tends to increase the SOW without correspondingly increasing the price.

• *Increases in direct costs*, such as travel. International projects often are victims of this type of cost variance. A small misjudgment can cause large cost problems.

The next most important variables in the management control system are the cost and schedule performance indexes (CPI and SPI) and the to complete performance index (TCPI) (see Table 7.1 for definitions).

The CPI, which is concerned with work performed to date, compares actual costs to budgeted costs. If the CPI is greater than 1.0, actual costs were less than budgeted costs, which indicates either that (hopefully) the work performance is more efficient than anticipated, or the budgeting process is flawed. A CPI of less than 1.0 indicates one of the following:

• Work performance is less efficient than anticipated.

• The time card recorded work against the project perhaps should have been credited against another effort.

• The budgeting process is flawed.

Each possibility must be considered to determine the correct reason for the variance. Thresholds should be set high for these indexes because correcting for variances can be difficult. The project manager should be concerned whenever the CPI less than 0.95 or greater that 1.05.

The SPI compares work performed to date with work scheduled to be performed to date, without regard to actual costs. An SPI greater than 1.0 is favorable. The work is ahead of schedule. An SPI less than 1.0 is unfavorable. The work is behind schedule. The reporting thresholds for this index should also be set high, for the same reason. Correcting even relatively small variances can be difficult.. As with the CPI, the report threshold should be set at 0.95 and 1.05, or even tighter. Unfavorable variances suggest the work is moving less efficiently than anticipated, as a result of either inadequate skills, poor planning processes, or improper time reporting.

It is crucial that the project manager monitor the administration of the financial management system to ensure that results are not biased by poor data input. The most important data inputs are the posting of labor hours against work packages and the estimates of work in process completed.

The TCPI looks at the other end of the schedule. Work still to be done on the project. It compares budgeted cost remaining (budget at completion [BAC] less budgeted cost of work performed) to the latest estimate of the actual cost of work remaining (latest revised estimate less actual cost of work performed). A TCPI equal to 1.0 indicates that the budget for the work remaining should equal its actual cost. If the TCPI is more than 1.0, the latest revised estimate (LRE) is probably overstated, meaning that the project could perform better than current estimates indicate. Conversely, a TCPI of less than 1.0 indicates that, unless performance improves, the LRE is understated and project profits will suffer.

Other indicators of the general performance of the project are the three estimates at completion (EAC). While these cannot be used in lieu of the LRE, they do predict the status of the remaining work on the project. Should an EAC exceed an established threshold, the project plans must be revised and a new LRE calculated.

The first estimate, EAC1, is calculated by dividing the BAC by the CPI. This will indicate any increase or decrease in the cost of the program and the amount of the project manager's reserve that may be consumed initially. If the CPI is greater than 1.0, a favorable condition, EAC1 will be less than the BAC. If it is greater than 1.0, there is a cost overrun in the making.

The second, EAC2, is calculated by dividing the BAC by the SPI. This will indicate any increase or decrease in costs resulting from adjustments in the schedule.

The third, EAC3, is calculated by dividing the remaining budget by the CPI, then adding the result to the ACWP (actual cost of work performed to date). If the CPI remains unchanged, the budget for the remaining work must be increased or decreased by the calculated amount.

USING THE VARIANCES

The indexes and variables calculated through reports produced by the financial control system are good at showing the status of the project's costs and schedule only at the point when they are calculated. Though the reports are accurate, the system is dynamic. Early in the project when there is little history, wide swings in the values of the variables are normal. As the project progresses, the movement of the values will lessen—but making changes in the project to affect those values will be increasingly difficult. For example, it might be impossible to absorb cost overruns in the superstructure of the Log Cabin Project and make up profits when all that remains to be done is the communications subsystem work. For that reason, it is important to implement the control system early and to take aggressive action immediately to correct problems and potential problems as soon as the system alerts the project manager.

The examples in Table 7.2 will explain how to use the variances to analyze the progress of the project. In each case, we'll look at the basic terms of the system: the BCWS, BCWP, ACWP, Schedule Variance (SV), and the Cost Variance (CV).

TABLE 7.2
VARIANCE ANALYSIS CHART

Example	BCWS	BCWP	ACWP	SV	CV
1	$X	$X	$X	0	0
2	$X	$0.8X	$0.8X	-0.2X	0
3	$X	$0.8X	$0.7X	-0.2X	+0.1X
4	$X	$0.8X	$X	-0.2X	-0.2X
5	$X	$1.2X	$X	+0.2X	+0.2X
6	$X	$1.2X	$1.2X	+0.2X	0
7	$X	$X	$0.8X	o	+2.0X
8	$X	$X	$1.2X	0	-0.2X
9	$X	$0.8X	$1.2X	-0.2X	-0.4X
10	$X	$1.2X	$0.8X	+0.2X	+0.4X
11	$X	$1.2X	$1.3X	+0.2X	-0.1X
12	$X	$0.7X	$0.8X	-0.3X	-0.1X

The table shows the 12 conditions that can exist among the three terms with BCWS held constant. The first example is the ideal. The BCWS = BCWP = ACWP and SV and CV both equal 0. Everything appears to be on schedule and on budget—the condition we all strive for.

There is one situation where this condition can exist but the project may not be in good shape. If there are too many tasks for which the WIP is measured by LOE, the report created will not indicate problems. That is why no more than 12 percent of the project effort should be measured by LOE. More can negate the integrity of the system. LOE tasks can be eliminated from the calculations to help avoid this ambiguity and represent the projects status more accurately, but that will affect the other calculations.

In the next example, both BCWP and ACWP are less than BCWS by 20 percent, making the SV negative but the CV = 0. The project is behind schedule. Since BCWP = ACWP, there is no cost variance, indicating that the work is being performed according to budget but the task is behind schedule as planned on the Work Package Planning Sheet. Since the work is being performed efficiently, this may suggest that staffing for the task is inadequate to maintain schedule. Another reason for the variance may be that required inputs from another task have not been provided, so a portion of the task cannot be started or completed. If the tasks are kept short, this situation can be avoided, leaving staffing shortage as the most likely reason for the negative schedule variance.

The third example takes this one step further. BCWP and ACWP are not equal, giving a cost variance. As before, SV = -0.2X, an unfavorable variance, but CV = BCWP - ACWP = 0.8X - 0.7X = +0.1X, a favorable variance for cost. This mixed result is not unusual. It indicates that the task is behind schedule but the work is being performed more efficiently than planned. The result is the same as in the previous example. The task is understaffed, but the favorable cost indication gives the manager the feeling that all is well because costs are under control and the schedule can be made up. That may be right, but the value of this system lies in the bad news, not the good. The project manager would be well advised to increase staffing to bring the task back on schedule as soon as possible. Otherwise, the schedule variance will cause an eventual cost variance.

Now consider example four, the case where ACWP equals BCWS, but BCWP is less than BCWS. There is a schedule and a cost variance, both unfavorable but equal. The project manager can be misled into thinking that the variances are entirely due to the schedule, since budgeted and actual costs agree, but a closer look makes it clear that they *do not* agree. The actual cost of work performed cannot be compared to the budgeted cost of work *scheduled*. The actual cost of work performed has to be compared to the budgeted cost of work *performed*. Here, actual exceed budgeted costs by 20 percent. The task is behind schedule and over budget, even if the time line indicates the budgeted costs have not yet been consumed.

Example five again assumes that ACWP is equal to BCWS, but this time BCWP is greater than BCWS by 20 percent. This time work on the task is being performed faster than planned and more efficiently. No corrective action is required, but it is clear that whoever prepared the WPPS took a more conservative approach than necessary—good information to keep in mind for future projects.

In example six, both BCWP and ACWP are larger than BCWS. SV = BCWP - BCWS = +0.2X, a favorable variance for schedule, and CV = BCWP - ACWP = 1.2X - 1.2X = 0.0X, no variance for cost. This assumes the project manager that though the task is ahead of schedule, it is being performed according to plan.

In example seven, BCWP is equal to BCWS, but ACWP is less than BCWS. SV, then, is equal to 0 and CV = BCWP - ACWP = 1 - 0.8 = +0.2X, a favorable cost variance. The work is on schedule and being performed more efficiently than expected.

In example eight, BCWP is still equal to BCWS but ACWP is greater than BCWS. Again, the SV is equal to 0, but CV = BCWP - ACWP, or X - 1.2X = -0.2X, an unfavorable cost variance. The work is on schedule but at the price of a cost overrun. It may be that (1) more people are working on the task than planned, (2) more senior staff are being paid more than planned, or (3) other direct costs, such as materials, travel, or temporary labor, are costing more than expected.

In example nine, BCWP has dropped below BCWS, while ACWP is greater. Both SV (0.8 - 1.0 = -0.2) and CV (0.8 - 1.2 = -0.4) are unfavorable. This should certainly grab the attention of even the most casual project manager. He's not only behind schedule but in an even more serious cost overrun position on this task. How serious the problem is depends on how critical the task is, and whether it's on or near the critical path for the project. In every case, this situation raises a red flag.

Reversing that situation is example 10. BCWP is greater than BCWS and ACWP is less. With an SV of +0.2 and a cost variance or +0.4, everything is looking good for the task.

When both BCWP and ACWP are greater than BCWS, and ACWP is greater than BCWP (example 11), the results change. The SV of +0.2 (1.2 - 1.0) is favorable but the cost variance of -0.1 (1.2 - 1.3) is not. The most common cause of this situation is the use of more resources or more expensive resources than originally planned, improving the schedule but at a higher cost.

In example 12, BCWP less than BCWS and ACWP is between the two. The SV = -0.3 (0.7 - 1), which is unfavorable, and the CV = -0.1 (0.7 - 0.8), also unfavorable. The schedule problem is serious. The cost problem may be less critical but it still needs attention.

The examples demonstrate how much information is available to the project manager who simply looks at the variances in cost and schedule for each of the CAMs as well as the project as a whole. All by themselves the variance reports show the project manager many potential problems and provide insight on how to analyze them. She can use that information, along with reports like the CPI, SPI, and TCPI, to design corrective actions to get the project back on plan.

One of the most common causes of cost variances in larger companies, those with over 1,000 employees, is the difference between the planned and actual cost of labor. In the planning phase, the pay rates for members of the project team are estimated, usually. on the optimistic side to make it easier to win the project. By the time the project is actually staffed, some of the team members will have been promoted and thus are more highly paid than originally estimated.

Assume that the project has only been underway two weeks, it's mid-January, and the CAM receives the first financial system reports. Although she knows that this early in the project, the reports will be less accurate than later when more data are recorded and bugs in the system are eliminated, it's still a good time to look for possible inaccuracies and see if any corrections to the financial control system may be required. The project manager's mindset at this stage is to improve the systems. She wouldn't normally expect to find problems so early. However, a problem exists.

Refer to Appendix A, Line Items 21 and 22.

For WBS Item AA2 (project documentation), there is a CV of -$2,000. The SV is $0. The CPI is 0.92, another indication of an unfavorable variance in cost. The SPI is 1.0, so the WBS task is on schedule, but the costs are not. The only task in work at that time is the systems specification, AA2.1, so the issue is with that task.

At first review, she determines that four people are working on the task, just as was planned. No overtime is recorded on the time cards for the period. Since everything appears to be in order and her mindset is on refining the reporting system, the CAM could easily overlook the fact that two of the four individuals are more highly compensated than was originally estimated.

Assuming, though, that the CAM *does* correctly identify the cause of the variance, the next common mistake is to assume, "That's OK because more experienced people will complete the task sooner." While this is often a valid assumption, the CAM must look at the facts to see whether it's valid here. In this case, it appears not to be, as evidenced by the SPI of 1.0. The task is on schedule, not ahead of schedule. With half the task completed, it is unlikely that the second half will improve sufficiently to make up the difference, so when the task is completed, the CAM is likely to be $4,000 in the hole, a negative cost variance that must be made up if her responsibilities are to be met. Also, unless the project manager takes some action to reassign personnel, the variance is likely to continue to grow at the rate of $1,000 per week.

Note that the CPI took a deep dive down to 0.92, which would normally get the undivided attention of upper management, but for the first few weeks of the project, the indexes can be expected to take some wide swings. After 60 days or so, the swings will be more modest, and the thresholds established for the indexes will become more meaningful.

This is not to say that wide swings early in the project should be ignored. They must be addressed, but not necessarily by senior management at this point.

In all cases, the project manager and the CAMs must do more than look at the reports. As shown in example one, there may be a problem with the measurements, not the variables. If the WIP metrics are faulty, the reports will not as accurate as managers need. However, if the defined tasks are kept short with none lasting over four weeks, the WIP will be accurate and the reports meaningful. Keep in mind that the early stages of planning significantly leverage the success of later project activities.

By studying the trends reported by the control system while applying the risk management processes described in the next chapter, the project manager can actively control the project, rather than reacting to adverse situations as they arise.

RECAPITULATION

Any commercial or even nonprofit firm must have a control system in place to make sure the company is headed where the leaders intend it to go. The control system must have:

- A means of measuring relevant parameters.
- A means of evaluating the significance of variances in the measurements.
- A means of altering behavior.
- A means of communication.

It will help the project manager get affirmative answers to these three questions:

1. Will the project be completed on time?
2. Will the customer be satisfied?
3. Will the project stay within budget?

Because the financial control system is related not so much to project finances as to management of costs and schedule, it is truly a management system, defined as a criterion-based control system.

The most powerful parameters of the system are the cost and schedule variances reported, along with the SPI and the CPI. Together they guide the project manager to and through problems and help keep the project on course.

The system is highly reliant on the proper selection and accurate reporting of the WIP measurements, but if these are indeed reliable, the system enables the project manager to actively control the project and prevent rather than merely react to adverse situations.

In the following chapter, you will be shown how to predict unforeseen events and control the risks on a project.

CHAPTER 8
RISK
MANAGEMENT

Risk is defined as the *possibility of loss*. Whether the project is commercial or nonprofit, there is the possibility that the profits or goals of the project will not be achieved. We add the phrase "due to unforeseen events" to relate risk to projects. For a project, then, risk is the *possibility of loss of profit or failure to achieve goals due to unforeseen events*.

To manage project risks means to try to foresee the unforeseeable, and then find a way to ensure that these unforeseen events do not adversely affect the project. At first glance, that task appears impossible, but there are effective ways to do just that.

I have seen many projects that have done a poor job of identifying risks and an even worse job of mitigating them. Because managers who normally deal in firm numbers find it troublesome to deal with uncertainties, they tend to be surprised at and unprepared for the (literally) unforeseen event when it occurs. Nevertheless, ambiguity is the natural situation for a project manager, and a risk of unforeseen events is just one more facet of that.

UNDERSTANDING RISK MANAGEMENT

Risk management systems are by nature subjective. Most of these "systems" boil down to someone's best guess as to the probability that any particular risk will occur, and to what degree.

The first concern—that the system is subjective—is not a valid complaint. Even a subjective system can give an accurate picture of project risks and help the project manager to evaluate, prioritize, and mitigate risks. It is less important whether the probabilities, or even the consequences, can be precisely defined. In this area, it is not possible to be precise. If it were, we could simply assign each risk a probably between 100 percent and 0 percent, then modify the schedule and budget accordingly.

The second concern—the best guess problem—can be alleviated with analysis. On two separate projects, I implemented a system that worked well. It allowed the project team to act either to prevent risks altogether or to have a fix in place in time to avoid serious consequences. If you stop at the "best guess" stage, you have not analyzed the risk, so you don't have a risk management program at all.

Some risks result in less cost than the cost of avoiding them. They can be suffered with little impact to the project—or just dealt with should they occur. Others can be a "show-stopper." They must be mitigated or eliminated in time to prevent severe damage to the project.

The two extremes are easy to identify, but it is also necessary to address those risk items that are between the extremes in a logical and prioritized manner. These are the ones that can become victim to the best guess problem when the risk management system fails to evaluate them carefully.

Risk management, in other words, is *a rigorous process of identifying, quantifying, and resolving uncertainties that might adversely affect the accomplishment of project objectives*. Early evaluation and detection of risk and execution of disciplined responses are critical to the success of both the risk management program and the project.

A risk management program has two aspects (1) planning and (2) execution. A plan to manage uncertainties requires a formal process of documenting, training, and continuous improvement. Execution consists of risk identification, assessment, analysis, and abatement.

Four basic types of risks or uncertainties that can affect the success of a project:

1. *Technical risk* is characterized by the uncertainty associated with new, unproved systems and the internal and external influences that can impact the performance or the availability of required functions. Although leading edge technological development may seem a typical example, more commonly technical risk refers to the performance of functional or operational requirements that may exceed the capabilities of the system chosen for the project.

2. *Schedule risks* derive from uncertainty about completing tasks in time to achieve key project milestone dates. Underlying causes of schedule risks are resource shortages, incorrect or incomplete schedule network logic, underestimates of task durations because of technical or development problems, and activities like tests the outcomes of which are uncertain.

3. *Cost risk* refers to uncertainty about meeting budgeted program costs. Cost risk usually correlates with schedule risk and performance—it depends primarily on underlying causes. Other possible sources of cost risk are optimistic estimates applied to areas of uncertain scope or significant technical risk and turnover of key personnel.

4. *Operational risk* refers to uncertainty in achieving the objectives or mission of the project. Recognizing system safety issues and their likely programmatic impacts is essential to items in this category. Risks of this sort are produced by implementing system requirements and specifications without thinking ahead about hazardous conditions that might ensue. They also arise from requirements that challenge the capability of the chosen approach to the system, or entirely new operational requirements that have not been achieved before.

Among other significant risks some projects might encounter are:

- The *risk that a product cannot be produced* because ability to devise methods and tools to implement designed items is not clear. This risk pertains to production feasibility. It often arises when it is necessary to the project to invent and fabricate new tools or materials. Typically, such a product has been produced in a laboratory by scientists and engineers but has not been fully tested in a manufacturing environment.

- The *risk that manufacturing and production processes cannot meet project demands* due to limitations in throughput, capacity, or quality of output. The company may be too small to meet production demands, or some unforeseen event might remove otherwise available capacity.

- The *risks associated with writing new software programs,* including functionality, documentation, language, ease of use by the customer, and size and utilization issues.

- The *risk that the system delivered is not supportable* due to logistics, training, software, facilities, or documentation limitations. The most common risk of this type is lack of critical repair parts, due, for example, to long lead times in production. The next most common cause is inadequate documentation hampering the ability to troubleshoot software or to conduct training.

- *External and environmental risks* are conditions to which the project may be vulnerable but are beyond the project manager's responsibility or control. Examples are government actions, executive decisions, labor actions, the business failure of a critical supplier, and *force majeure* events.

THE RISK MANAGEMENT (RM) PLAN

The RM plan documents the structure, methodology, and organizational accountability of the RM program. It applies to all members of the project team, the Risk Management Board (discussed below), company management, the customer, and any integrated product teams (IPTs). (Though there are many whole books that describe IPTs, basically these teams simply consist of all the skills necessary to produce a product of high quality, on time, and to a customer's satisfaction. Any of the subsystems of our Europistania Log Cabin Project is a candidate for an IPT.)

Early in the project, risks will appear greater as technical issues are exposed. They will become more realistic as estimators gain experience in expressing uncertainties. The process described in the plan will foster an aggressive approach to identifying, re-examining, and resolving new risks throughout the life of the project, because assuredly risks will continue to be identified throughout the life of a project, especially an international project.

The Risk Management Board (RMB) advises the project manager. Because its members must have a high degree of experience, it is composed of the managers of each of the major subordinate activities of the project. RMB members should include representatives from company and project management, technical leadership, engineering specialties, IPTs, and similar projects in the company.

The RMB assigns responsibility for each risk identified and evaluates and approves abatement plans for each. The RMB should meet weekly, and the meetings should be open to any member of the project team who has an interest in any risk.

The documents associated with the RMP are:

- *Risk management program plan,* which defines the structure, organization, responsibilities, and procedures for managing project risks.

- *Risk abatement plans,* which document the mitigation of risks the RMB assesses as "high" or "medium."

- *Risk management status reports,* when required. They are submitted to describe RMB actions, individual risk status, and progress under the abatement plans.

- *Risk register or log,* a record of all RMB dispositions with a detailed history of each risk from identification to closure.

- *Risk watch list,* an abbreviated version of the risk item log containing only risks that the RMB is actively monitoring.

RISK MANAGEMENT BOARD (RMB) TOOLS

The RMB requires both performance data and risk management tools. The tools available, which range from personal judgments to simulations, fall into two general categories: (1) deterministic and (2) probabilistic.

Deterministic methods use single-value estimates to describe the variables. These estimates can be as best guesses or averages. Basic financial spreadsheets and most scheduling tools are limited to a single-value entry that approximates the judgment of whoever provides the information. The advantage of these tool sets is that they are familiar and available to all team members so learning curves are short and changes are easily implemented. The disadvantage is that such estimates are imprecise. Also, because the data are arithmetically summed, any bias is compounded so that errors are obscured. Risk-averse estimators may build unnecessary cushions. Risk-takers may underestimate the resources required. These problems can be remedied somewhat by setting aside a contingency or buffer augmented by best-case and worst-case scenarios and the interactive review of experienced team members.

Probabilistic (also called *stochastic*) approaches are designed to account for uncertainty. Estimates of values are presented as ranges. Their advantage is that expected values, such as dates, durations, resource requirements, and costs can be estimated using simulation models to obtain a numerical assessment of possible impact on project objectives.

The disadvantage is that applying these tool sets requires specialized training and use of the results requires thorough understanding of the models used. Taken out of context, without this understanding, the findings can be severely misleading, which undermines the value of the approach. The project manager must be conversant with the model used so that he can use the results obtained effectively.

Project risk models can capture and test project variables, usually expressed in terms of cost and schedule, and subject them to Monte Carlo modeling. Especially effective on large projects, Monte Carlo sampling techniques generate output distributions of durations, dates, and costs. Whether designated dates, milestones, and other scheduled events are achievable can be inferred from the model's results.

In drawing up the PERT chart of the Integrated Master Plan, the optimistic, pessimistic, and most likely values of duration described fit a specific distribution. Software tools can take these distributions, measure the sensitivity of each variable, and determine the probabilities of achieving schedule and cost goals.

Moreover, multiple critical paths with varying degrees of criticality can be compared to determine the likelihood of achieving schedule and cost goals for each path.

Work performance data, in the form of cost and schedule information, are used in all phases of risk management. The data are used to identify possible risk items associated with the WBS elements, as well as inputs to either of the two approaches discussed. Any risk abatement effort will be measured against the same elements.

Trade studies are the most effective way to preclude risks. Evaluating alternative approaches to a design or implementation concept, taking into account all technical, cost, schedule, and operational aspects of each approach, will prevent or alleviate many risks beforehand. (How to conduct trade studies is covered in Chapter 11.)

Project metrics are effective predictors of the risks associated with problem areas. The threshold standards for each metric should be established so that hitting them will trigger RMB interest and action. This is especially important in software projects, where adverse data trends may be the only early warning indicator available.

Selection of tools and software programs will depend on the characteristics of the project and each risk to be analyzed. The RMB will determine the type of information required to evaluate and act on each risk.

The basic flow shown in Figure 8.1 can be applied to each element of the WBS to identify each risk, compare assessments of the status of a risk over time, and evaluate risk abatement procedures.

Once there is a plan, the Risk Management Program can be executed. This takes place in four distinct phases: (1) identification, (2) assessment, (3) analysis, and (4) mitigation. The whole process from plan through execution is shown in Figure 8.2.

As the project progresses, the actual results and continuous evaluation will provide corrective information to support changes. Where project resources are limited, they can be allocated against the risks that are most likely to impact success. Throughout the life of the project, the search for new risk items is continuous; and monitoring and measurement of mitigation actions is iterative.

FIGURE 8.1
RISK MANAGEMENT PROCESS

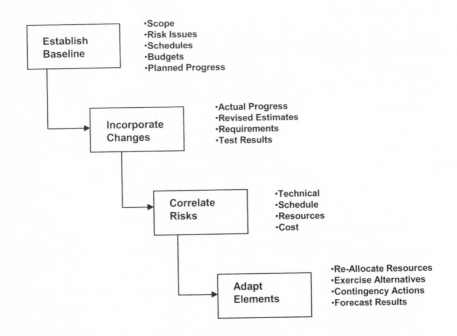

FIGURE 8.2
RISK PROCESS FLOW CHART

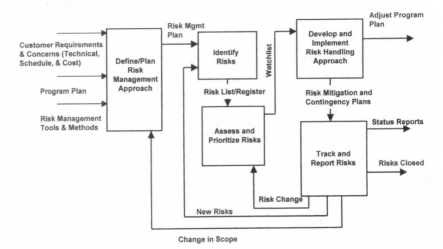

As can be seen from Figure 8.2, beginning on the left, inputs to the RMP are the project plan, customer concerns, and any risk management tools and methods that will be used. From the plan, members of the project team, as well as others, identify which risks the RMB should evaluate and prioritize first. These constitute the Watch List prepared for periodic review by the RMB.

For every item on the Watch List, an approach must be defined to handle, mitigate, or eliminate the risk. Progress on the approaches will be reported periodically to project and upper management.

Sometimes, the project plan or the scope of the project may have to be adjusted or changed, but usually the risks will simply be closed as mitigation actions are completed.

THE MITIGATION PROCESS

The first step is to identify the specific risks. Continuously throughout the project each WBS task must be reviewed for potential risks. A risk candidate can arise from any number of sources and any member of the project team. Risk sources other than the WBS might be:

- *Working sessions* designed to record concerns and problems. Both technical and managerial meetings typically can have such a purpose.

- *Design reviews.* The purpose of a design review is to confirm good aspects of the design and identify faults and problems, whether they are micro or macro. Any fault may represent a risk, and the ensuing discussions may expose additional risks.

- *Internal management reviews.*

- *Brainstorming sessions.*

- *Modeling results.*

- *Project metric reports.* Adverse trends are certain indicators of problematic elements.

- *Customer comments.* Few things are more embarrassing to a project manager than a customer (or a boss!) who expresses a concern that turns out to be correct—especially if she was initially ignored.

- *Cost and schedule data*, especially estimates to complete.

- *Concerns* of experienced people within the company.

The project manager must be alert for anything that may represent a risk to the project and insist that each be evaluated for the need for mitigation activities.

RISK IDENTIFICATION FORMS

To make it easier to identify risks, the project should draw up a Risk Identification Form (see Figure 8.3).

The top of the form records basic information about the risk to facilitate its tracking:

- The name given to the risk.

- The risk level assigned.

- The risk number assigned.

- The originator (the person identifying the item as a risk).

- The assignee (the person assigned to monitor it).

- Date submitted to the RMB.

- Last date reviewed.

- Date the risk is likely to occur.

- Date the risk should close.

- Date it actually closed.

- Whether the risk is internal or external.

- Date of the last update.

The next block explains the risk and how it might affect the project. This should be a concise statement of why this item is thought to be a risk.

The bottom half of the form contains the calculations needed to find the probability of occurrence (Pf), the consequence of occurrence (Cf), and the risk factor (Rf), which is what determines the level of risk inserted at the top of the form, which in turn determines how much attention this item will command.

FIGURE 8.3
RISK IDENTIFICATION AND STATUS

Risk Level

Risk Number   Originator   Risk Assigned to:

Date Submitted   Date Reviewed   Date Risk Will Occur   Date Risk to Close   Date Closed   Internal or External Risk?   Last Update

Definition of the Risk and the Baseline Document

Probability of Occurrence (Pf)   Consequence of Occurrence (Cf)   Risk Factor (Rf)

Cost Level Cf   Discussion of Cost Impact

Schedule Level Cf   Discussion of Schedule Impact

Technical Level Cf   Discussion of Technical Impact

Operational Level Cf   Discussion of Operational Impact

Determination of Cf

Cost	Schedule	Technical	Operational	Level
< 1 % of TC	< 10 days	low perf, minor chgs	Degraded	Low (1-3)
< 5% of TC	< 30 days	low perf, mod chgs	System Threat	Med (4-6)
> 5% of TC	> 30 days	Unaccep perf, maj chgs	System Failure	High (7-9)

Determination of Rf

Rf = Cf X Pf

High, Rf > 5.5
Med, 5.5>Rf>2.5
Low, Rf < 2.5

Not only can a risk item be identified from almost any source, any "what-if" question raises the possibility of a risk. Especially early in the project, each such question should be given attention. Most will be rejected on initial assessment, but none should be ignored.

The person who identifies a risk item provides the narrative for the Definition and Baseline Document block, as well as a short discussion of each type of risk that might be related to the item—cost, schedule, technical, operational. The baseline document may be the contract, the specifications, or the SOW—whatever contains the requirement that is at risk—the specific requirements paragraph should be referenced. The opinion of the person identifying the risk about the probability of occurrence should also be sought because that person probably has a good idea about how likely it is to occur. Once completed, the form is submitted to the RMB for assessment.

The person identifying the risk may or may not be the assignee responsible for monitoring the risk item. It depends on whether that person is the one most knowledgeable or best qualified to monitor progress of the item. In every case, only the most qualified should be assigned that responsibility (see Appendix B for a set of completed forms for the sample).

Assessment of each risk is a continuous process, performed in relation to the project as a whole, not just an individual task. The initial assessment is largely subjective because there will be little data on hand to support a more objective review. It estimates the value of the consequence of occurrence to the project. At the bottom of the Risk Identification Form are listed project-unique criteria for the values of Cf. For instance, under Cost, a consequence of less than 1 percent of total project cost is listed as low consequence, with a value of 1 to 3, depending on how much less than 1 percent the Cf is (1 percent is arbitrary, selected for illustration only). If the potential profit on the project is on the order of 15 percent to 20 percent, however, 1 percent of total cost might well constitute medium or even high consequence. In practice, a dollar figure should be used rather than a percentage. In any case, the selected value of Cf for cost, 1 through 9, is placed in the Cost Level block at the left of the form.

A similar assessment is done for schedule impact, with less than 10 days considered low, 10 to 30 days medium, and more than 30 high. Critical to the threshold value is the time associated with contractual penalties. The Cf value for schedule is then selected and placed in the Schedule Level block at the left of the form. The process is repeated for technical and again for operational impacts, and those values are placed in the appropriate blocks at the left of the form.

The highest number of the four consequence levels is placed in the Cf block in the center of the form and that value is used to calculate the Rf. For this Cf value, it is not appropriate to average the consequences because that obscures, understates, the actual potential consequence of the risk item.

Each time this risk item is reviewed (how often will be decided by the RMB), the assessment is adjusted. With each assessment, confidence in the integrity of the system increases.

Analysis and continuing assessment of the risk requires additional data in the form of performance and historical information, and sometimes more sophisticated modeling. The RMB determines the need for data and assigns team members to collect that information for it. As more is known about the item, the probability and consequence of occurrence can be refined, enhancing confidence in the evaluation and improving the credibility of the Risk Management Program.

For every risk item with an Rf of high or medium, the RMB must create an action plan. Those with a low Rf will be dealt with case by case, because often the cost of mitigation exceeds the consequence of the risk. But even low-risk items must be monitored periodically to ensure that none has grown into the medium or high category.

ACTION PLANS

The next form needed is one on which to record the Action Plan leading to mitigation or abatement of each risk (see Figure 8.4).

Risk abatement alternatives fall into one of three general categories:

1. Avoidance. An alternative or backup approach is chosen.
2. Prevention. Resources and other corrective actions are applied to the existing process so that the adverse impact does not occur.
3. Assumption. It is decided to accept the possible consequences. This choice is made only for low-risk items and only after careful RMB deliberation.

FIGURE 8.4
ACTION PLAN STATUS

No.	ACTION PLAN	STATUS	COMMENTS		
			ASSIGNEE	DUE DATE	
			ASSIGNEE	DUE DATE	
			ASSIGNEE	DUE DATE	
			ASSIGNEE	DUE DATE	

Risk Number ☐   Risk Level ☐   Last Update ☐

At the top of the form, basic information is recorded for the specific risk being addressed—name of the risk, number assigned, Rf assigned, and date of the last status update. The form has space for four action plans to be recorded. If more are needed, additional sheets can be attached. Each plan is described with its latest status, the name of the assignee, and the due date for closure of the plan (not the risk).

The action plan is a series of steps leading to one of the three abatement approaches. Each step has an assignee and a due date for a status report to the RMB. The steps may be serial, the second beginning after the first is completed, or parallel, with all or any combination of steps conducted simultaneously. Whatever the situation, the action plan must be aggressive. It must also be completed before the risk is expected to occur.

A risk item is closed only after it no longer poses any danger. The uncertainty has passed, the risk abatement procedures have been implemented successfully so that there is no longer any risk, or the RMB decides it has moved to the "low" category.

RISK LOG

The Risk Management Program relies on one more form, the risk register or log, which has as a subset the watch list. Both use the same form, but the watch list contains only risks that the RMB is actively monitoring.

Figure 8.5 sketches a suggested risk log.

On the form, risks are listed numerically as they are accepted by the RMB without regard to the level of risk. Basic information for each risk is recorded—level, name, whether it is internally or externally generated, concise definition, who is responsible for tracking, when it was submitted, when it is expected to occur, when it is scheduled to close, and when it actually closes. Once closed, a risk is no longer active.

The watch list of risks actively monitored by the RMB includes all high and medium risks and any low-risk items that may be of interest to management.

FIGURE 8.5
RISK LOG

PAGE 1 of ___

No.	Level	Title	I/E	Definition	Assigned to	Submitted	Will Occur	To Close	Closed

THE FLIP SIDE

The same process, reoriented, can be used to identify and evaluate opportunities for the project. Typical is the possibility of expanding the contract to cover more work and thus possibly increase profits, or creating a follow-on project. Opportunity items can be identified just as risk items are, and assessment and valuation of an opportunity can be determined much as the consequences of risks are evaluated.

The project manager should look only for opportunities that directly relate to the project, with a view to making it more profitable. Opportunities that are external to the project should be delegated to another company organization to pursue so that the project manager is not diverted from his primary responsibility.

RECAPITULATION

The processes required for a Risk Management Program are:

- *Identify a risk.* The item can originate from any number of sources, such as management meetings, informal discussions, design reviews, or status meetings. Once it is identified, the administrator assigns it a risk number and records it in two places. The first is an entry to the project risk log (or register) and the second is its own Risk Identification and Status form, where the originator fills in some basic data about the risk, giving it a common name for easy reference. The originator then completes the Definition of the Risk and the Baseline Document block on the form and should open the Discussion block of the Consequence section.

- *Assess and prioritize the risk.* The RMB, at either a scheduled or an ad hoc meeting, reviews the risk, its description, and its Pf, placing their initial judgment on the value of Pf in the appropriate block. The RMB may then either accept the description as written or ask for a better explanation. The board determines the cost impact should the risk occur, does likewise with schedule, technical and operational impacts, and assigns Cf values for each based on the quantitative values provided by the form, writing the values in the appropriate blocks. The largest value of Cf is copied into the block in the center of the form, and the risk factor (Rf) is determined by multiplying Pf by Cf. The result is used to determine whether this is a low, medium, or high risk value based on the criteria in the lower right block of the form (see also Appendix B). If it is medium or high, the risk is assigned to someone who is responsible for monitoring the risk and reporting regularly on its status, updating the project risk register.

- *Prepare risk mitigation plans.* Mitigation actions recorded on the Action Plan Status form for each risk may fall into any of several approaches. Most plans will require some research to determine how real the risk is. That will also help to adjust, if necessary, the Pf previously assigned. Some action plans may be designed to eliminate the risk, such as by identifying backup suppliers or recruiting more experienced personnel. The action plans must also incorporate contingency plans covering what will be done should risk abatement fail. Examples might be work-around activities or using outside help. Any number of impact-minimizing actions are possible.

- *Track and report risks.* Monitor the effectiveness of the action plans, modify them as necessary, prepare status reports for management, adjust the risk status as more information comes in, add new risks as they appear—and, if necessary, change the scope of the project.

As risks are mitigated, opportunities may be identified to enhance profits. The primary difference is in the actions taken. In this case, the challenge is to ensure that the opportunity does happen. The forms would be modified to reflect the differences in goal, but the administrative processes would be similar to those of risk management.

The next chapter surveys the Six Sigma System of Quality Management and describes tools from the Six Sigma "toolbox." Applying that system to a project will also help the project manager to avoid risks.

CHAPTER 9
METRICS AND QUALITY MANAGEMENT

One of the challenges for nonmanufacturing businesses has been to improve their processes to better satisfy customers, reduce costs, and keep owners and stockholders happy with earnings. I say "nonmanufacturing" only because in manufacturing, there are numerous repetitive processes that lend themselves to analysis and improvement. Whereas in a different environment—like the one-of-a-kind project represented by the Europistania Log Cabin Project—opportunities for improvement are more difficult to identify. Even in manufacturing firms, many processes not directly associated with the assembly line present the same difficulties.

If you want to improve something, you must first be able to measure it. If you want to improve customer satisfaction, for instance, you have to determine where you stand at the moment, and what you have to do better to improve customer satisfaction. Finding the appropriate metrics is not easy.

For years, businesses have been measuring performance data and establishing industry benchmarks with metrics like return on investment, return on net assets, sales per square foot, and sales per employee that help measure how well the business is performing. Measuring performance is clearly not a new idea.

But measuring performance of internal processes, and finding ways to improve them, is new. At least, an approach involving teams, management, and other stakeholders in the process is new.

Quality control systems have similarly been around a long time, from the Zero Defects ideas of the 1960s with their "do it right the first time" philosophy to the current ideas of measuring employee and organization performance with the goal of continually improving all processes. Jack Welch's successes at General Electric fueled the next evolution of quality management with the Six Sigma movement.

Zero Defects was created to ensure that a particular defense contractor would complete a government project on time, with no significant errors. Project-oriented, it required each employee to pay strict attention to ensure that he did every job correctly and that no re-work was required. The effort was successful for particular projects, but subsequent applications failed to perform to expectation.

The lessons learned from that and from the later Japanese approach of total quality management were eventually incorporated into the continuous measurable improvement concepts of the Six Sigma quality system. That system requires management involvement in and direction of quality management, taking it away from independent and isolated quality control departments and making it a corporate-wide mission for all employees.

Those with a working knowledge of statistics know that sigma, represented by the lower case Greek letter σ, represents a standard deviation in the distribution of a population (of anything). Six Sigma stands for six standard deviations, a near perfect condition. If the number of defects is in the 6σ range, you are very near zero (99.9997 percent accuracy), through not literally "zero." It is a challenging goal but often achievable.

BASICS OF SIX SIGMA

The three Six Sigma basics are:

1. Goals.

2. Themes.

3. Defined roles.

GOALS

The lofty goals of the Six Sigma system can be simply stated:

• Improve customer satisfaction.

• Reduce the costs of internal processes.

• Improve the profits of the corporation.

For a project like the Europistania Log Cabin Project, the manager has few opportunities to rate or improve customer satisfaction. A low number doesn't lend itself to statistical analysis, and any following project will likely have a different set of requirements. Customer satisfaction will be measured by how well the project team meets the contract requirements. There is no need to assign a Six Sigma team to measure that, but it could be necessary to assign one to study the causes of any failures to meet specific requirements and to design processes to ensure that the failure is not repeated.

Any project consists of numerous tasks or processes. Performing them quickly and efficiently improves cost and earnings data for the project. The Six Sigma system of quality management described briefly below makes that easier. If you choose to apply Six Sigma to your project, organization, or company, there are many sources that go into full detail.

Six Sigma has its own terminology and vocabulary. Though I have tried to avoid buzzwords, this is one of the disciplines where using the terminology of the practitioners is unavoidable.

Six Sigma is more than a standard quality control system, and one of its most visible characteristics is the involvement of management at all levels. However, though upper management drives, supports, and rewards the system, the ideas for improvement originate within the Six Sigma teams formed to solve problems. The teams are, and must be, empowered to initiate changes that improve the process under study. At the same time, unsuccessful initiatives must be an acceptable part of the process. Teams must be allowed to "fail" on occasion, because taking initiatives is necessary. If a team is afraid of reprisals for failure, its members will stop offering new ideas, and Six Sigma will fail.

THEMES

- *Theme One: Focus on the customer*. Performance measures must be based on how they will affect the customer, as are recommended improvements.

- *Theme Two: Management decisions are based on facts and data.* By basing decisions on facts and data rather than emotion or "gut feel," specific problems can be identified, analyzed, and permanently resolved. Before decisions are made, the manager has to ask, "What do I need to know to make this decision, where can I get the information, and how can I use it to best advantage?"

- *Theme Three: The process is the key to success.* Mastering the processes of a business is the key to building its competitive advantage and delivering value to the customer.

- *Theme Four: Management must be proactive.* Rather than reacting to the business environment, Six Sigma encourages management to take action before something happens.

- *Theme Five: Collaboration must be without boundaries.* Jack Welch attributes much of his success at GE to his mantra of "boundary lessness." Internal disconnects and competition rob businesses of billions of dollars, whereas these organizations should be cooperating toward common goals.

- *Theme Six: Drive for perfection, but tolerate failure.* When you are striving for perfection, some ideas will not work. People who are afraid of the consequences of failure will not make that last heroic effort to achieve perfection.

DEFINED ROLES

For a variety of reasons, some of the roles defined in the literature for the Six Sigma system carry martial arts names, such as Green Belt, Black Belt, and Master Black Belt. Others have more traditional names like Sponsor, Champion, or Leader. Yet, others have taken on catchy titles like Grand Poobah, Chief Sigma Officer, and VP of Six Sigma. The advantage of new names for a new quality management system is that the names carry no baggage left over from previous quality control systems. The role names and definitions are:

- *Green Belt.* The Green Belt is trained in Six Sigma skills, sometimes to the same level as a Black Belt, but does not act as a fulltime team leader. He may be assigned to a team as a member where he works within his normal job assignment.

- *Black Belt.* The Black Belt is often the Six Sigma team leader, responsible for training, guiding, controlling the dynamics of the team, and keeping the effort moving toward success. These are usually people in middle management who serve for a specified period of time, usually 18 to 24 months, and have been trained in all the Six Sigma skills.

- *Master Black Belt (MBB).* The MBB is the coach and mentor for all or a group of the Black Belts. An expert in Six Sigma skills and analytical tools, he should possess a background in engineering or an advanced degree in business. An MBB provides executive guidance for the Six Sigma teams.

- *Champion or Sponsor.* These terms are often used interchangeably, but sometimes a Sponsor is assigned to supervise several Champions. The role is to ensure that the Six Sigma projects are aligned with the overall goals of the enterprise, advise the leadership team, obtain the necessary resources, conduct "tollgate" reviews, and negotiate conflicts.

- *Implementation Leader.* Often a corporate vice president, and usually the quality executive, the implementation leader is at the top of the Six Sigma hierarchy. Her goal is to drive Six Sigma thinking across the organization, encourage use of the tools, and strengthen corporate habits that support the Six Sigma goals.

THE TEAM LIFE CYCLE

Each Six Sigma team is formed to address a specific problem, find a solution, and make it last. Accordingly, the team has a finite life cycle defined in six phases, as follows:

1. **Select the Project.** Management usually chooses the problems that are candidates for a Six Sigma Team but sometimes a team is formed to identify candidate projects for study. Each problem must be definable, meaningful, and manageable so that a solution can be developed. The problem has to be understood by everyone participating in the effort, and solving it must be a business necessity—otherwise, work on it is a waste of time and money. It also has to be manageable—small enough that it can be addressed without overwhelming the team. A problem that is too large has to be broken down into smaller, more manageable, pieces.

2. **Form the Team.** The first decision is which Black Belt or Green Belt will lead the project. The leader must be someone familiar with the problem, knowledgeable in the technology associated with it, but not so involved as to have been part of the problem himself. The remainder of the team are those members of the IPT or those responsible for the process or task.

3. **Prepare the Charter.** The charter is a written guide for the team. It contains the reason for pursuing the problem, the goals, the strategy, a basic plan, and the scope of the effort. It may also define the responsibilities of the team members. The charter should be a collaborative effort of the entire team.

4. **Train the Team.** Six Sigma emphasizes the need for training, which will normally take from one to four weeks, usually interspersed with periods of work on their regular jobs. The training is on the DMAIC process (standing for *define, measure, analyze, improve,* and *control*), which is discussed in the next section.

5. **Perform DMAIC and Implement the Solutions.** Teams are expected to draw up project plans, training, and procedures for finding solutions, and are responsible for implementing and measuring performance of the processes they propose.

6. **Hand off the Solution.** Eventually, the team must break up and the members return to their normal job assignment. At that point, the new process becomes the responsibility of the official Process

Owner, who has the responsibility to sustain the gains achieved by the team. The Process Owner is a member of management, perhaps as high as a Vice President, who has overall responsibility for the specific process throughout the organization.

THE DMAIC PROCESS

The DMAIC process is the standard process for the Six Sigma teams to address problems. It has five steps:

1. *Define the Problem.* Facts must be used to define the problem and its effect on the business. To say merely that "the customer is not happy with our service" is not defining the problem. To say that "only 85 percent of our deliveries are on time" or that "we've met only 90 percent of the customer's 'desired' requirements" is only the beginning of a definition of the problem. To define it, we still need to know why and under what conditions we failed to meet the customer's expectations. For this we need a high-level diagram of the process currently used to meet the customer's demands.

2. *Measure.* The next step in the process is to collect data to help quantify the problem (or the opportunity, for that matter). Using the diagram created in the first step, the team begins observing and recording facts and numbers that offer clues to the cause of the problem. Six Sigma training is required to understand what and how much data are required to quantify the problem. Six Sigma Black Belts are skilled in data collection.

3. *Analyze.* The analysis step begins by melding experience and data measurements and then reviewing the process. An initial hypothesis is formed about causes of the problem. As more data are gathered and compared with the hypothesis, it is tested, refined, or rejected as a root cause of the problem. This continues with new hypotheses until the root cause is identified.

4. *Improve.* This step is the beginning of the solution. It is also the step most teams are tempted to jump to on day one. That's the way we're conditioned. We see a problem, we solve a problem. It is, however,

premature to start this step until the previous three steps have been completed. Premature action toward a solution may cause the team to solve a problem that doesn't exist, or create a solution that is no better than the problematic process being addressed. Improvement begins with the team members proposing solutions that eliminate the root cause of the identified problem.

Once several potential solutions have been proposed, the analysis begins anew. Costs and benefits have to be weighed to determine which solution would be the best approach. Once one is chosen, the Champion or the leadership team makes a decision about whether to do it based on the analysis and recommendations of the Six Sigma Team.

An approved solution is then given a small-scale trial, or pilot, to see what could go wrong. The employees who will use the new process will have to be convinced that it works. Their cooperation is critical for collecting data and tracking any improvement. After any necessary adjustments identified by the pilot, the process is put into effect throughout the organization.

5. *Control*. Left alone, employees will return to their old habits. In the control step, the team must continue to persuade employees of the benefits of the new process, ensuring that the process is followed until it becomes the new habit for the employees. In this step, data are collected continuously to measure actual improvement from the new process and to determine whether other adjustments should be made.

THE BASIC TOOLBOX

The "toolbox" contains a set of specific tools that have been identified as key to helping Six Sigma teams successfully understand, manage, and improve a business or a process. Other tools that are similarly effective could be added to the toolbox. Any in-depth discussion of the tools is beyond the scope of this book, and in fact requires specialized training, but here is an overview.

BRAINSTORMING

Brainstorming is not new. It is used not only in Six Sigma but also in the Risk Management Program and anywhere a new and imaginative approach is needed. The term refers to a free-flowing discussion of possible solutions or problems without regard to the feasibility of the ideas presented. This tool is used frequently in a number of phases of the Six Sigma process.

Though apparently common, brainstorming is not as simple as most people seem to think. Few people are adept at it unless they have been trained in the technique.

Ideas resulting from brainstorming are categorized for further review, with the Six Sigma team voting to determine which survive. Affinity diagrams are commonly used to categorize ideas and prioritize them.

An Affinity Diagram is a creative process, used with or by a group to gather and organize ideas, opinions, and issues. The purpose is to add structure to a complex issue by breaking down the issue into broad categories and gaining agreement among the team. The process is:

- State the issue or problem to be explored. Start with a clear statement of the problem or goal and provide a time limit for the session—usually about 45 minutes is sufficient.

- Brainstorm ideas for the issue. Each participant should think of ideas and write them individually on index cards or sticky notes.

- Collect the cards or sticky notes, mix them up and spread them out (or stick them) on a flat surface such as a desk or wall.

- Arrange the notes into related groups. Allow a few minutes for the participants to pick out cards that list related ideas and set them aside until all the cards are grouped.

- Create a title or heading for each grouping that best describes the theme of each group of cards.

STRUCTURE TREE OR TREE DIAGRAM

A structure tree (see Figure 9.1) is used to show the links between ideas. A specific idea, for instance, may have two parts. The two parts of a service problem with telephones might be (1) disruption of service and (2) the slow restoration of service. Each of those two might have further subsets, which can be visualized through a structure tree.

FIGURE 9.1
STRUCTURE TREE

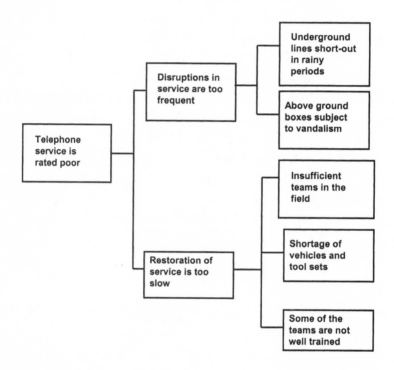

SIPOC DIAGRAM

An SIPOC (supplier, input, process, output, customer) diagram (Figure 9.2) is a chart used to show the major processes incorporated into any business activity. It is handy to help define the boundaries and important elements of a process without detail that could add to confusion in the early stages of problem-solving process.

The SIPOC chart shown in Figure 9.2 shows the acquisition and installation of logs for the Europistania Log Cabin. It obviously is a high-level process chart that shows the process without getting into too much detail. It can help the Six Sigma team visualize what is part of the process and what is external and therefore not of interest to this team.

FIGURE 9.2
SIPOC DIAGRAM

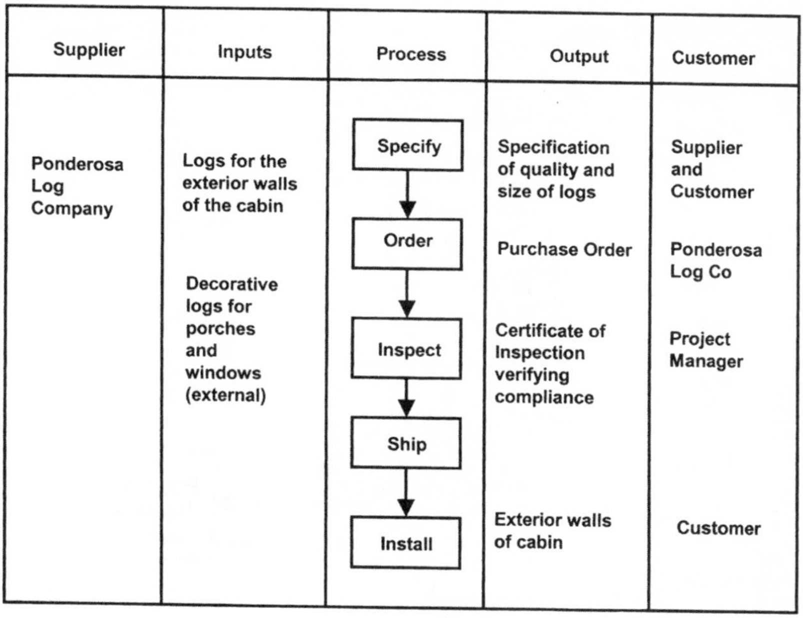

Supplier	Inputs	Process	Output	Customer
Ponderosa Log Company	Logs for the exterior walls of the cabin	Specify	Specification of quality and size of logs	Supplier and Customer
		Order	Purchase Order	Ponderosa Log Co
	Decorative logs for porches and windows (external)	Inspect	Certificate of Inspection verifying compliance	Project Manager
		Ship		
		Install	Exterior walls of cabin	Customer

FLOWCHART

A flowchart goes into more detail about the process, including the tasks, decision points, and feedback loops. Taking another example from the Europistania Log Cabin Project, Figure 9.3 shows the flowchart of the request to the Department of Commerce (DOC) for an export license.

For those unfamiliar with flowcharts, begin at "START" and go to the first process, which is to review the DOC Commercial Control List (CCL). The decision point is Yes, the items you are concerned with are on the list, or No, they are not. The decision is made item by item, so there may be several yeses and several noes. If the decision is No, the next step is to proceed with purchase orders for the items. If it is Yes, the next step is to submit the request for an export license to the DOC.

The next decision is whether the items on the list are approved. If they are, take the path to "prepare purchase order." If not, return to engineering for redesign, after which the redesigned items go through the entire process again until each can arrive at "END."

FIGURE 9.3
FLOWCHART FOR AN EXPORT LICENSE

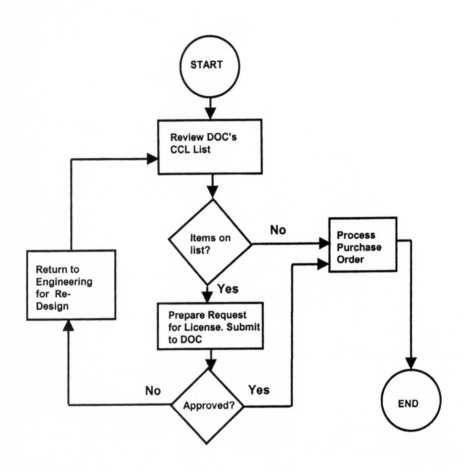

FISHBONE CAUSE AND EFFECT DIAGRAM

This diagram (see Figure 9.4) is effective in brainstorming sessions. The chart is easily created during discussions by putting the problem in the last block to the right, then putting potential causes at the ends of each "fishbone." The diagram is expanded as causes of the causes are discussed. Clearly, the diagram can become busy rather quickly. If it does, it means the problem needs to be further dissected.

FIGURE 9.4
FISHBONE DIAGRAM

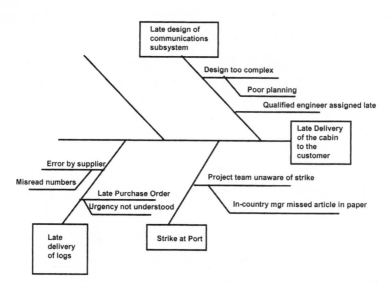

A fishbone diagram cannot prove the real cause of a problem but it does expose many possibilities (hypotheses) for later consideration. The strength of these diagrams is the visibility they give to the process under study, and the fact that they guide the team members to identify all the possible causes of the problem. In addition, they help identify critical variables to be measured and data that will be required to analyze the problem further.

DATA-GATHERING TOOLS

Data-gathering is a science of its own. Each of the many techniques has inherent errors, unless huge resources in time, money, and personnel are expended in gathering 100 percent of the possible data. Sampling—taking a specified percentage of the available data population—is one technique for controlling the cost of data gathering. Sampling results can be amazingly accurate, but there can also be errors.

When collecting facts and data, it is first necessary to define what is to be collected, when, and under what conditions to make the data consistent. A number of techniques classified under Voice of the Customer (VOC) methods, can help an organization collect customer input and feedback, among them sophisticated market research methods, requirements analysis, data mining techniques, and data warehousing. Once data are available to the team, analysis can begin. Among the techniques in the Six Sigma toolbox for analyzing the data gathered are:

- *Process Flow Analysis.* Using a flowchart of the process under scrutiny, the team can identify unnecessary steps, potential bottlenecks, unclear decision points, and meaningless reworks. This approach, one of the most valuable analytical tools in the toolbox, is also one of the quickest ways to find clues about root causes.

- *Value-Added Analysis.* One of the advantages of focusing on the customer is that it enables the team to look at the *value* of a process, or a step in the process, to see if each step does indeed add value.

A number of years ago when I was an Artillery Officer on active duty in Germany, our battalion was reassigned from the intermediate headquarters of an artillery group to report directly to VII Corps Artillery. While we were under the group's command, our headquarters was required to submit a total of 28 reports per month on a wide variety of subjects. I inquired of our new command which of those reports were required. While awaiting an answer, I submitted only the reports required by Army Regulations—five.

Apparently, those five were sufficient, because none of the other 23 were ever mentioned. This is an extreme case—23 monthly reports and no value added.

Processes in place for a long time tend to expand by adding checks, reports, extra analyses, and any number of activities that for the most part add nothing of value *to the customer.* Eliminating these extra steps can often improve the process. But that isn't the place to stop improvement. Who can say that the original process, before all the unnecessary steps were added, was itself efficient? It, too, needs to be analyzed.

Although some people can quickly gain meaningful information from a printout consisting only of numbers, most of us can understand the data more easily if we can see a picture. A huge variety of charts and graphs can be used to depict data in visual form. Pie charts, Pareto charts, histograms, trend charts, and scatter plots are all useful for displaying data in a way that furthers the analysis.

For most processes, the tools discussed so far are sufficient to find and correct the root cause of problems. When they are not, Six Sigma teams can use such statistical methods as regression analysis, tests of statistical significance, or one of the many design-of-experiments methods, but statistical results are rarely "black and white." It often takes experts to explain their meaning, as has been demonstrated often in courtrooms where lawyers try to explain the statistical significance of a DNA test result. Nevertheless, statistical analysis of well-developed data has a great deal of credibility.

IMPLEMENTATION

Once the Six Sigma Team has a solution to recommend, the final step in the Six Sigma process is implementation. This requires good management planning, organizing, executing, and controlling skills. A miniproject is usually formed to manage this phase of the effort. As with any other project, the manager has to look at what could go wrong (risk analysis) and how to prevent or mitigate it. The best way to keep things from going wrong is using the Risk Management Program (Chapter 8) to predict what could go wrong and then taking action to ensure that it does not.

Each new process must be documented and employees trained to use it. After the process is in place, more data must be gathered to ensure that the improved results continue, and to find other problems to be addressed.

The goals at all times are to improve customer satisfaction, reduce cycle time, and reduce defects and their costs in our deliverable products. Though not always easy to implement, a Six Sigma approach to quality management can pay huge dividends. For international businesses, this is particularly important because of the strong competitive position of companies from other countries. To continue to survive, we must strive always to be the best in class. Six Sigma gives us the means to continuously improve.

RECAPITULATION

To improve anything, there must be a way to measure it and define a benchmark. Today, businesses have progressed beyond the traditional measures of business performance to a focus on impact to the customer. The Six Sigma Quality Management System has three goals:

1. Improve customer satisfaction.

2. Reduce costs.

3. Improve profits.

In addition to having a customer focus, management is well-advised to base its decisions on facts and to be proactive in process improvement. In their drive for perfection, managers must be willing to tolerate failure in order to encourage ideas outside the normal boundaries.

Roles of Six Sigma team members include:

• Green Belt.

• Black Belt.

• Master Black Belt.

• Champion or Sponsor.

• Implementation Leader.

The six phases in a Six Sigma lifecycle are:

1. Select the project.

2. Form the team.

3. Write a charter.

4. Conduct training.

5. Perform DMAIC and implement the solution.

6. Hand off the solution to the process owner.

The single most important process in Six Sigma is DMAIC, which stands for define, measure, analyze, improve, and control, but there are numerous tools in the Six Sigma toolbox to help the team in the DMAIC process.

International projects have a number of aspects absent from domestic projects. One of the more important, offsets, is covered in the next chapter.

CHAPTER 10
OFFSETS

One way international projects differ from domestic projects is their exposure to offset requirements. Offsets is a term used for the requirement that the contracting company reinvest a portion of its revenues from the project in the economy of the host country. Offsets have become a widely used vehicle for governments to reduce the impact of imports on their economies.

UNDERSTANDING OFFSETS

Although offset obligations have been around a long time, in recent years countries have been much more aggressive in demanding that American firms that do business in their country reciprocate by investing in the local economy. Though historically applied only to defense contracts, they are now also common in large construction projects and increasingly in other commercial ventures.

Offsets are imposed for both economic and political reasons but they are used primarily to lessen the impact of large outlays of a country's hard

currency by having much of the money returned in an economically beneficial form. Offset requirements may, for instance, oblige the contractor to
provide meaningful work for local firms or to buy specified amounts of
goods and services in the host country. They create local jobs and improve
the technology of local industry, but, as we shall see, they can also have a
negative impact on the United States. Large projects—those greater than
US $10 million—almost invariably contain offset requirements, but small-
er projects can be exposed to these obligations as well.

The original RFP and IFB documents will notify potential bidders of
the need to include an offset plan any proposal submitted; the customer will
evaluate the offset plan along with the proposal for the project.

The offset plan can be an important part of the marketing effort for a
project. The in-country representative will be able to advise the project
manager about the offset in general and even whether a particular approach
is likely to be a winner. Because a superior offset proposal can often win
the project even if another proposal for the primary project is better, attention to the offset plan is as important as attention to the project.

> One large defense project in Saudi Arabia for approximately $3 billion
> required a 100 percent indirect offset—an investment of about $3 billion in
> Saudi Arabia. That limited the number of companies able to bid on the con-
> tract to a very small number of very large defense contractors. The winning
> offset proposal incorporated a variety of infrastructure-enhancing projects,
> from truck factories to roads and communications facilities. Even though a
> competitor's technical proposal was rated superior to that of the winner, the
> offset aspects carried the competition.

Offset requirements can run the spectrum from trivial to as onerous as
the one in the Saudi Arabia example, from quite a small percentage of the
entire project up to 100 percent. I have never heard of an offset exceeding
100 percent, which would in any case seem inconsistent with the purpose
of the offset. Note that, contrary to first impressions, big offsets, though
troublesome, do not necessarily prevent a company from making a profit
because the offset investment can also generate profits. Try maintaining an
equity position in the enterprises formed by the offset.

DIRECT AND INDIRECT OFFSETS

Offsets come in two forms, direct and indirect. Through *direct* offsets the customer receives a work share or an advanced technology directly related to the contract, typically by sharing in the production of the item contracted for under license or by providing services related to the contract. Indirect offsets include investment and counter-trade agreements. The required investment may be in an industry unrelated to the primary project or for transfer of technology unrelated to the project to the host country. Either form of offset sends work overseas and creates a foreign competitor for American products and services.

Depending on the motivations of the customer, direct and indirect offsets might be weighted differently. For example, a direct offset program might be awarded dollar-for-dollar credit against the obligations, whereas an indirect offset might require several dollars investment before the company can be credited with one dollar against the obligation.

At one time, it was possible to satisfy offset requirements simply by flying on the host country's airline, staying in local hotels, and buying supplies in-country. Today, the contractor has to consider investments of value, so-called "noble work." Because offset contracts often call for transfers of technology, the U.S. government gets involved through export licenses and technical assistance agreements. And, as we know, getting the necessary export authorizations can add as much as six months to the contract schedule, or even a year if you count the time for the customer to approve the document, taking into account negotiations of the final versions between your own company, the customer, and the U.S. government. That may be rare, but it's not so rare that I haven't experienced it.

For a project in Portugal, the contractor was certain that the technical assistance agreement would be approved because the export of hardware had already been approved, so he began work on the project. However, the customer disagreed with the wording of the agreement and refused to sign. Work on the project had to be stopped, at great expense, while negotiations continued. It took 11 months to resolve the issues with the customer before the request could be resubmitted to the Department of State.

In some countries, requirements for direct offsets specify that the company must export *from* that country products of similar technology to those supplied to the country. In the case of joint ventures, they could be the same products supplied in the first place. The clear purpose of such a requirement is to open up the lucrative American market to that firm, creating a direct competitor for the American manufacturer.

The defense industry has through its many offset programs transferred an economically significant number of jobs overseas that might otherwise have stayed on our shores. The impact extends beyond the normal bounds of projects and of the defense industry. The Bureau of Industry and Security, which monitors offsets suggests that when an American furniture company loses a bid to a South Korean firm, an American defense corporation may well have helped the foreign firm secure the furniture sale as a part of a military offset obligation.

Governments have been expressing concerns about offsets since the 1950s. Though these expressions continue today, other than preparing reports reflecting the negative impact of offsets, not much has been done to limit them. On the positive side, companies that sell cars in the United States have been required to build factories here to satisfy offset requirements.

United States rules on licenses and protection of patents are strict, but their enforcement overseas is not. The international business community is replete with stories of designs stolen during execution of an international contract.

Putting aside the pros and cons of the offset concept, if a contract like the example of building the log cabin in Europistania carries an offset obligation, the company will have to honor it, lose the project, or possibly suffer penalties later in the project. No matter how tempted you might be to resist, it's better to wage the battle with letters to your Senators and Representatives. The immediate and pragmatic need for the project will necessarily override any philosophical concerns about offsets and transfer of jobs overseas.

SATISFYING OFFSET REQUIREMENTS

Offset requirements can be satisfied in a number of ways. The use of local subcontractors, for instance, directly benefits the project while satisfying the obligations. It has the added benefit that the project team can oversee the offset effort without needing additional dedicated resources from the company.

Another approach is to form a joint venture with a local company in which the money invested satisfies the offset obligation. The profits from the joint venture would be shared as agreed in the contract forming the venture. This requires a separate organization from that of the project team, but once it is approved by the customer, the project manager is relieved of those concerns—unless the manager of the offset effort is a subordinate. The main reason for this arrangement would be to control the interface to the customer. A joint venture also mitigates the cost of the offset by a profit-sharing arrangement within the joint venture.

Whatever approach is anticipated, the customer must be involved before the final decision is made.

Some countries require that a bidder open an offset account before proposals are evaluated and the contract awarded. They have learned that many companies fail to follow through on offset obligations. The winner of the competition for the project may then apply the offset account against the obligation. This is one way a bidder can demonstrate that the offset proposal is credible, which can give an advantage over the competition. While there are obvious risks to this approach, future bids on projects in that country could realize a benefit from the investment even if the immediate competition is lost. Two countries that encourage this approach to enhance (though not guarantee) a company's chances of winning future business are Turkey and the United Arab Emirates (UAE).

Dealing with an offset obligation can be either a good or bad experience, depending on how creatively the manager responsible meets the challenge. In international (and for that matter, domestic) business, as in poker, whether you win or lose depends on how you play the hand that's dealt.

The approach that the project manager of the Europistania Log Cabin chooses is to hire subcontractors and labor in country, using only Americans only as supervisors for the overseas phase of the project. He also plans to buy 20 percent of the material the project needs in-country.

RECAPITULATION

Offsets are a fact of international business life. They are part of the requirements in many contracts. An offset plan is often required as a section of a proposal. Their purpose is to offset the outflow of hard currency resulting from the contract.

Offsets can be either direct or indirect. If they are direct, they are associated with the contract itself. An example is the requirement that a portion of the contract be performed by local subcontractors. Indirect offsets require investment in the economy outside the project defined by the contract.

Any offsets that require a transfer of technology, such as software products, are subject to a form of export license referred to as a technical assistance agreement. Export licenses are issued by the U.S. Department of State.

Among the many ways to satisfy offset requirements are hiring local subcontractors, buying materials locally, forming joint ventures, and issuing licenses for production of patented products. Other ways are limited only by imagination and mutual agreement of the parties.

The next part of the book deals with executing the project in-country. The first chapter of the section tells how to select and manage local subcontractors.

PART III

EXECUTING THE PROJECT IN-COUNTRY

CHAPTER 11

SELECTING AND MANAGING SUBCONTRACTORS IN-COUNTRY

Selecting a subcontractor in a foreign country can be difficult and risky. It is of course easier if the subcontractor has a track record with the company on previous projects or such a grand reputation in the required discipline that the project manager can feel totally confident in the subcontractor's capabilities and responsiveness. That rarely happens in the international arena.

Ideally, if the project is successful, similar projects in the same country or region will follow. If the selection of local subcontractors on the first contract produces mutually satisfactory relationships, the selection process for later projects will be much easier. After all, one of the reasons for taking a company international is to expand the business and create international relationships to facilitate future business abroad. Still, there is a potential disadvantage. The downside of finding a good local subcontractor is possibly creating an in-country competitor for your core business.

PROS AND CONS

There are a number of reasons managers of international projects find it advantageous to hire local subcontractors, among them:

- Hiring locally is a condition of the contract.

- It is part of the offset plan.

- It's cheaper to hire local firms than a U.S. company.

- Local firms are likely to be familiar with local regulations, standards, and license requirements.

- They are expert in the local language.

- They can help the company deal with customs requirements.

- They are a source of temporary skilled labor.

In many countries, probably most of those in the industrial development phase, there is a motivation to gain technical knowledge from firms based in the United states and other industrialized nations. That transfer of technology is usually accomplished through subcontractors who gain operational and technological knowledge as they work on the project. They are often granted licenses to otherwise protected processes. The project manager is encouraged to help train these subcontractors, and may be granted concessions for doing so in the form of relaxed schedules or, far more rarely, additional funding.

If the customer directs the selection of the subcontractor, as is common in certain parts of the world, the project manager will find it hard to exercise control. As the customer's choice, the subcontractor can be more independent than is conducive to a well-run project. Worse, if the subcontractor doesn't perform, the project manager has little recourse. Though there is always the option of not accepting a contract with such a stipulation, that may not be the best course to follow if the company is interested in foreseeable future projects in that country.

Fortunately, as happened in all but one case I've seen, placing technical or managerial assistance with the subcontractor will help keep the project on track. In that one exception, the subcontractor would not accept inplant assistance or even much guidance, but eventually the project was completed successfully because a diplomatically skilled engineer found ways to provide the necessary guidance indirectly.

The project gains financial advantages from the use of local subcontractors from both the lower cost of the local company and the savings gained from not having to relocate U.S. personnel. Because wage rates for skilled professionals are generally much lower in other countries than in the United States and Europe, a local company can make an acceptable profit off a lower price than would be adequate for an American company.

My experience with local subcontractors has been positive. Each one I've worked with had the knowledge and skills to perform the tasks required. In most cases they did not have use of the higher technology tools to which we've become accustomed, yet they were nevertheless able to do the job on time.

A common task for a local subcontractor is to provide a flexible skilled labor force to replace labor that would otherwise have to be sent from the United States, though not normally on a staff-day for staff-day trade. The significant cost savings from not having to relocate so many people to the host country, however, have to be compared to the potential added costs of possibly having to lengthen schedules and the costs of training the subcontractor in the management control system used, as well as implementing the system. Still, with the universal use of the Internet, much of the extra administrative load can be alleviated.

At the same time, knowledge of local customs, regulations, and licensing requirements may make it possible for the local subcontractor to complete tasks on the project with fewer risks to the schedule than would be the case for an American subcontractor or in-house staff that do not have such knowledge. A local subcontractor, for instance, can often help delays in port related to clearing customs because of frequent dealings with the customs officials and more intimate knowledge of local bureaucratic processes. The subcontractor may also be able to help the project manager source materials locally, an even better way to avoid customs problem. The trade-off is thus not merely in terms of labor rates but in terms of the total costs of using or not using local subcontractors.

MAKING A CHOICE

Once the decision to hire a local subcontractor is made, the next challenge is how to select the right one. The project manager begins the process by defining precisely the work to be accomplished, the standards of quality expected, and the schedule that must be met. She must prepare an RFP incorporating a model contract with a detailed statement of work—all written, of course, in simple declarative sentences, because that style of writing is more easily translated than complex sentences with multiple verbs.

There are likely to be at least two candidates, each with its own strengths and weaknesses. It is rare to find a clear-cut winner that obviously stands out above the rest.

Hiring a local subcontractor is a classic case of decision-making under conditions of uncertainty. The decision involves a large number of factors, perhaps more than one decision maker, multiple attributes, and an uncertain outcome. Textbooks covering decision-making under uncertain conditions offer many approaches to addressing the problem, but the relatively simple model proposed in the following paragraphs will yield valid results.

Assuming that the project manager, not the customer, has the option of selecting subcontractors (which, though not invariable, is the norm) he will have to draft criteria that define the requirements to be met and help ensure the selection of the best candidate. The specific technical criteria will vary depending on the nature of the project, but some general elements must always be considered. I think of it in terms of gates the candidates must get through:

- The first gate is price. Each candidate must offer a price that is within range for negotiating an acceptable price for the work. Those outside the range—unable to get that gate open—are immediately rejected from further consideration.

- The second gate is whether the candidate company has the capacity, the skills, and the staff to do quality work within the schedule. This is a gate because all candidates must meet this criterion.

- The third gate is whether the candidate company is acceptable to the customer. Though the customer will often claim to be disinterested and avoid any responsibility for the selection, it is always a good idea to inquire.

Once candidates get through the three gates, the project manager must compare them by asking a series of questions:

- Is the company big enough for the project? Will the project be too significant a portion of its annual sales, placing the candidate at risk?

- Is the company adequately financed to do the job without an unreasonable up-front payment?

- Can the company acquire any necessary but missing skills in time?

- Has the company been in business a long time? Has it been in the business for which it is a candidate a long time?

- Does the company have a track record in the work to be done?

- How good is the company's reputation in the industry?

- Does the company have a reputation for honesty? Are there any indications of unethical business conduct? *Unethical* here is defined by U.S., not local, standards of business ethics.

- Will the working relationship be pleasant? Or contentious?

- Does the company appear to have a tendency toward litigation or arbitration?

- Will communications with the company be easily understood? Are there likely to be language difficulties?

- Will the principals be accessible to the project manager?

- Is the company certified to ISO 9000 standards? Does it have a good quality control system? How independent is the quality control function?

- Does the company have automated information systems that are compatible with the project?

Using these or similar selection criteria to supplement the responses to the RFP, the project manager will often find that it comes down to choosing the one that seems to be better than the others "all things considered."

To interview representatives of the candidates who make the final cut, the project manager should form a small advisory team of people with different points of view representing a variety of disciplines. At a minimum, the team should consist of project manager, contracts manager, in-country manager, and technical lead, supplemented by people from other areas that are appropriate for the situation. Having an evaluation team helps to ensure that nothing is missed during the discussions and that all the criteria get careful consideration while the normal biases of individuals are contained. But the role of the team is to advise the project manager, to make sure every important element is considered, not to assume his responsibility for the final selection.

Should the number of candidate subcontractors warrant it, you can use a weighted value analysis to help identify the best candidate. Each criterion is assigned a number, the size of which indicates the relative importance of that decision element. (Criteria identified as gates are not included because every candidate must get through each of those unweighted.) The most important criterion for this particular project could be assigned a value of 10, the least important a value of one. More than one element may be assigned the same value, as is shown in the worksheet in Table 11.1.

TABLE 11.1
SELECTION WORKSHEET

Selection Criterion	Total Points	Candidate One	Candidate Two	Candidate Three
Company size	10	8	6	7
Company financing	10	7	7	8
Availability of skills	8	8	6	5
Time in business	7	5	6	7
Track record	10	5	7	9
Reputation	9	7	7	7
Record for honesty	9	6	5	7
Relationship environment	6	6	4	3
Litigiousness	8	7	4	4
Communications	7	7	5	6
Meet ISO 9000	8	8	8	8
Information technology	8	8	6	5
Totals	**100**	**82**	**71**	**76**

Each member of the evaluation team fills in a worksheet for each candidate, assigning points for each criterion, which may be anywhere in the range from zero to the total number of points allotted to that element. After all forms are completed, the totals from each team member would be summed or averaged to determine the relative standing of each candidate. Ultimately, the totals will point to the candidate that, "all things considered," appears to be the one favored by the consensus of the team.

Why isn't price included in the evaluation? Because price was used as a gate, all candidates are at least within negotiating range. The weight put on price, which would clearly be heavy, would unjustly favor a low price over the other factors—and, too often, the candidate with the lowest price is the least likely to perform the task successfully. That's why it's better to rank the candidates first before adding price to the equation. Once they are ranked, you can see whether any differences in price are justified by difference in capabilities. Then, negotiate the selected candidate's price.

Clearly, the key to the validity of this methodology is in the choice of selection criteria *and* the relative value assigned to each. While a consensus is used to determine those values, the project manager will apply his own judgment, based on experience, to approve or modify the consensus values arrived at.

The time and resources required for the selection process must be included in the Integrated Master Schedule. More than one subcontractor may be needed, and candidates may have to be interviewed more than once, so it may take more than a single trip to the site to conclude subcontractor agreements. These must be completed in time for the subcontractors selected to begin work on the date the schedule calls for.

Failure to appreciate how much time it takes to reach agreement with subcontractors is a common reason the first in-country schedule slips. It is best to have the contract in place well before the work is scheduled, even if the subcontractor has to wait until you are ready for him. A strong Integrated Master Plan will remind the project manager when the decision must be made and give the information necessary for timely completion of the process.

THE MANAGEMENT CHALLENGE

Managing a subcontractor located in a foreign country can be more difficult than managing a domestic subcontractor for a number of reasons. First,
the principals may not be accustomed to the criterion-based management
systems we take for granted—systems that use rigorous metrics to measure
progress, require variance reports and analyses, and set out detailed plans
to maintain the scheduled and budgeted progress. Second, the local culture
will affect how the subcontractor's management relates to the people within that company as well as to project management. As one of the managers
at The Aerospace Corporation in El Segundo, California, once told me, "It
takes a wee bit of Irish wit and charm" to manage an organization from
another culture.

The best way to get the best out of a subcontractor is to make sure its
principals completely understand the requirements and to maintain excellent communications with them. An environment of mutual trust and
respect where all are working towards the same goals goes further than any
sophisticated management control system. A well-prepared SOW is the
first step towards achieving complete understanding. Most companies, like
most people, want to do a good job. They just have to be told what the other
party considers a "good job," that is, what is expected of them.

One element of the contract must be that the subcontractor abide by the
management control system implemented on the project, making the necessary reports and conducting the necessary reviews to function as a full
member of the integrated project team. Typically, a subcontracts manager
is assigned to ensure that the requirements of the agreement are met, and
that the subcontractor gets paid as agreed, but though that person can help
administer the project controls, in the final analysis all decisions remain in
the hands of the project manager.

A subcontractor who is unable or unwilling to participate directly in the
financial control system—and there are many legitimate reasons why this
may be so—must nevertheless report progress on the assigned tasks regularly in a way similar to that required of the CAMs. He can be given report
forms or formats for doing so in ways that do not cause his organization
undue inconvenience. Tasks assigned under his Work Breakdown Structure

should be short, and the start, work in process, and completion of each task must be reported. Most important, as prime contractor, the project manager must have a way to verify those reports.

A carrot-and-stick approach is valuable in controlling local subcontractors. Speaking of sticks first, stiff penalties for late or unsatisfactory task completion helps ensure on-time (or near) delivery of high-quality work. The weakness of the stick approach is the time involved in notifying the subcontractor is he is late or his deliveries are unacceptable, the time needed to make recovery, and the time it takes to apply penalties. There may also be other significant damages consequential to these delays, and it is rare for those damages to be assigned to the subcontractor, so even the penalties imposed may not make up for the damage done to the project.

Along with the penalties, therefore, think about carrots, such as incentives for early delivery. Incentives benefit subcontractors in two ways:

1. They are pure profit and therefore eagerly sought.

2. A shortened schedule means lower costs for the subcontractor, another source of improved profits, and may help the project schedule by adding some slack.

In my experience, too many organizations overlook this inexpensive and effective method of improving the probability that a subcontractor will complete work satisfactorily and on time. Incentives that are about half the size of the penalties are usually sufficient motivation for excellent performance.

Another attractive incentive, should your company plan future projects in the same country—and that was one of the goals—is a long-term relationship in which you agree to give that subcontractor a right of first refusal to participate on future projects. However, if you do establish such a relationship, your company must honor it, and the manager of the next project will have to plan within that constraint.

Payment to subcontractors on the project must be conditioned on performance. The initial payment should be as small as can be negotiated and subsequent payments tied to events selected as critical to the schedule. As long as the subcontractor meets his commitments, he remains cash positive.

The risk in this method relates to the financial stability of the subcontractor. Should negative cash flow create a survivability problem, you might find yourself in the position of having to finance him, buy his company, or find another subcontractor at a most inopportune time.

Another method of controlling subcontractors that is not to be overlooked is using the customer as leverage. There is a high probability that there is a business relationship between the customer and the subcontractor, but even if there is not, it is highly probable that the subcontractor would like to have such a long-term relationship with a customer in the same country. Note, though, that while there is leverage that can be applied here, it's in the nature of a "silver bullet." You can use it only once. Using it more than that will adversely affect your relationship with the customer.

A control method to be avoided in international projects is the threat of litigation. Even if it were effective, which is rare, at a minimum, this heavy-handed approach undermines the relationship. Moreover, you're operating on unfamiliar ground, with uncertain results, and in his legal environment. If the owner of the subcontracting company turns out to be the brother-in-law of your customer, the results may be more negative than you could possibly anticipate.

RECAPITULATION

Selecting a subcontractor in another country can be both difficult and risky. Still, there are a number of reasons that the project will be induced to hire local firms, all related primarily to contractual necessity or cost-benefit analysis.

To reduce the risks associated with selecting a subcontractor, it is necessary to have some method of evaluation and prioritization among candidates. Whatever criteria are used for selection, before they are all candidates must pass through at least three gates:

1. Price within an acceptable range.

2. Capacity, skills, and staff to do the job.

3. Acceptability to the customer.

Once selected, the subcontractor must be managed. The project manager must both deal with the customs and cultures of the country and ensure there is a way to measure progress that will mesh with the certified progress system for the project as a whole.

A carrot-and-stick-approach that uses both incentives and penalties is an effective means of controlling the subcontractor. He is in the business for a profit, so incentives offer an opportunity for an increase in expected profits. A system that affects subcontractor cash flow is also effective. Tying payments to specific important milestones so that subcontractor cash flow is positive milestones are achieved and negative if not is an effective way to maintain the overall schedule.

The following chapter describes how to conduct trade studies to support buy decisions, selection of alternatives, and other decisions that must be based on substantial amounts of information.

CHAPTER 12
TRADE STUDIES

Every commercial venture, like every other human endeavor, involves decisions over which of the possible approaches to take. Which approach is best and what makes it best are questions that recur regularly. Most decisions we face can be resolved with the knowledge gained from our personal lifetime experiences and education. Decisions about more complex problems, however, require disciplined analysis to sort out the relevant facts and arrive at the optimal course of action.

Trade studies are sometimes required by contract. Every major defense and large commercial contract will require trade studies to determine the best approach to solve issues of concern to the customer. Their scope and the issues to be addressed will be including in the RFP. Often the contract will specify that the results must be included in the systems design review, typically about 90 days into the project. Certainly, if that is too soon for results, at least the design of the study will have to be presented to the customer by then.

ELEMENTS OF A TRADE STUDY

Trade studies can run the gamut from single-page fact sheets to complex position papers ("white" papers) to volumes of analyses and conclusions. Regardless of their relative complexity, though, every trade study will contain five basic elements:

1. Statement of the problem.

2. Facts relating to the problem.

3. Necessary assumptions.

4. Selection and evaluation of alternative approaches.

5. Conclusions and recommendations.

DEFINING THE PROBLEM

The first step is to define the problem to be addressed. What do we want to know? What results do we need to get? If the problem is not adequately defined, the wrong question will be studied and the results will be inconclusive. That's why the first element of a trade study is the statement of the problem.

As simple as it may sound, an accurate statement of the problem to be resolved is the key to a successful trade study. One of the most common trade studies is to resolve a make-or-buy-decision, but to state the problem as "Is it better to make the product or to buy it?" is too open-ended. What is the real issue? Is the decision political, e.g., does it have marketing implications? Is there an offset requirement, or will buying the product satisfy one? Is it a question of employing engineers, or of manufacturing capacity or scheduling? Is it cost? Is there an internal quality problem? Why does this a problem have be addressed by a trade study?

In other words, the problem statement must be specific so that the study will resolve the real problem. Otherwise, the study may conclude a "make" decision is appropriate due to lower costs, whereas the underlying problem is not so much cost as the risks associated with scheduling the manufacturing. Such a problem might be stated as "Do the risks associated with manufacturing schedules justify a buy decision?"

The problem is always stated as a question. The conclusion of the study answers the question, detailing the rationale for the answer.

GETTING THE FACTS

The second element of a trade study is listing every nontrivial fact associated with the problem as stated. Note that the facts must bear directly on the problem, so that extraneous bits of data that will not help resolve the problem do not complicate the process. Gathering the data relating to the problem is done just as is the data-gathering related to Six Sigma approaches described in Chapter 9.

There is a danger that the list may include assumptions. That temptation must be resisted. Historical records of manufacturing schedules are facts, for instance, but extrapolating them into the future becomes an assumption, not a fact. It is a fact that the previous manufacturing runs of this product have been late, but it is an assumption that such delays will continue into the future. Facts outweigh assumptions when approaches to solving the problem are evaluated.

MAKING NECESSARY ASSUMPTIONS

Though assumptions should not be confused with facts, some assumptions do have a bearing on the problem. It is at this point that all the factors that will weigh on the decision that are not facts are listed, applying the same rules as for listing facts. The assumptions must be nontrivial and they must bear directly on the problem under study. A typical assumption that is nontrivial is the level of risk that has been estimated to inhere in a given decision.

The two lists, facts and assumptions, merit the attention of everyone working on the trade study or with a stake in the results. All should review the lists so that they can be fine-tuned and to ensure that the facts and assumptions listed are properly stated and do have a significant bearing on the problem. No stakeholder should be able to object *after the conclusion of the study* that "the basic assumption is flawed." That is a clear indication that the list was not sufficiently fine-tuned. It is also an indication of how important this step is in the conduct of the study.

OPTIONS FOR ACTION

The fourth element of a trade study is listing viable alternatives or approaches to be considered. At this point, brainstorming and other Six Sigma tools are effective ways to identify alternatives. Some trade studies are designed from the start to address a choice between two specified alternatives, but if the original problem is adequately bounded, the number of alternatives will in any case usually be limited to no more than two or three. If as many as five are identified, the problem must be restated more precisely to narrow its bounds.

For our sample problem, the alternatives appear to be only two—make the product in plant or buy it from outside sources. But here is a potential third choice—combining the two options, buying some of the product and manufacturing the rest. This third choice is within bounds if the problem has to do with the risks of manufacturing delays and the purchase of a few items might mitigate that risk sufficiently.

However, *which* source to buy from is *not* within the bounds defined by the problem statement. If the decision is to buy, from whom is the next decision and will require analysis of the available suppliers. That would give rise to a new trade study with a different set of facts and assumptions to consider.

The approaches selected for consideration need to be distinct and discernable. An endless set of choices with minor variations is possible but to be avoided.

In its simplest form, evaluation of options consists of comparing facts and assumptions to see which of the alternative choices has the most favorable "pros" and the least damaging "cons." The result should be a short fact sheet that describes the rationale for selecting each approach. Even uncomplicated trade studies have merit because they record the rationale for certain decisions. They are also normally required by the quality management system, which periodically reviews the decision-making processes of the company and its project teams.

More complex trade studies can easily become small projects with their own staff and schedule. Gathering the data associated with such a problem is more difficult. It may require more use of the Six Sigma tools. Selection and evaluation of alternatives, if not carefully defined by the problem statement, may also prove difficult enough to require more sophisticated tools.

Often such complex trade studies require simulation and mathematical modeling, especially when the project is a defense contract. Modeling and simulation require specialized skills and tools as well as large-capacity computer facilities.

The need for trade studies is identified during proposal preparation. Determining which approach to include in a proposal, whether because it is required or to counter the rationale of the approach it is assumed a competitor will take, will require a trade study before the proposal is even submitted. These often complex trade studies produce position papers that may be used by the marketing team to advocate an approach or test customer response before the proposal is submitted.

Trade study requirements are not unique to U.S. defense contracts. In my own experience, customers in three different countries requested on-site field experiments, and I am aware of other projects with similar requirements. Each experiment lasted three to four months with up to two more months required to analyze the data and prepare reports.

In the international arena, you also must assume that the competitor will obtain a copy of any study that addresses an approach for the proposal and will attempt to discredit the study any way possible. If he is successful, it will also discredit your whole proposal. Keeping the study out of the hands of the competitor, though best, is rarely successful. Making sure the study is valid and unbiased will counter most efforts to discredit the conclusions.

Trade studies required by contract are always complex. The only reason the customer has offered to pay for them is that his own organization is incapable of conducting them. That doesn't mean that it is incapable of evaluating a study, however. The studies not only require a miniproject organization, they require schedules, budgets, and periodic reports, both oral and written. Because the results will be input to some element of the project plan, study activity is included in the project's PERT chart, perhaps even on the critical path.

THE FINAL STEP

The last step of a trade study is presenting the conclusions and recommendation. The conclusions are a concise statement of the strengths and weaknesses of each approach evaluated. The recommendation is the study group's collective judgment, its consensus, on which is the best course of action. The conclusions should be presented in a side-by-side chart to show clearly how the alternatives compare.

Most upper-level managers I've briefed over the years prefer to see only the final recommendation, without bothering with the comparison, but a manager who must decide whether to approve the study results and accept the recommendation should see the alternatives compared so that he can make an informed judgment about the results.

RECAPITULATION

Trade studies can result, depending on their complexity, in simple fact sheets, thorough white papers, or volumes of data and conclusions. Regardless of the complexity, there are essentially five elements to any trade study:

1. Statement of the problem.

2. Facts relating to the problem.

3. Assumptions about the problem.

4. Selection and valuation of alternative solutions.

5. Conclusions and recommendation.

The carefully detailed statement of the problem in the form of a question is critical to the direction of the study. Getting the facts may require anything from a sophisticated data collection effort to a simple list of pertinent facts.

Assumptions are used when there are not enough known facts on which to base a solution. Managers making assumptions are cautioned to remember that assumptions are not facts, and to make sure that any assumption made relates directly to the problem.

Brainstorming is one excellent method of identifying viable alternative solutions to a problem. Other Six Sigma tools can also be used here, as well as during the analysis phase.

Finally, the study team must publish its conclusions and recommendations for management review. Showing the alternatives and the criteria used to prioritize them can help management either accept the team's recommendation or to select another.

In the next chapter, the final one, I bring everything together with explanations about working the problems and working the program.

CHAPTER 13

WORKING THE PROJECT, WORKING THE PROBLEMS

Successful international projects can give a major boost to company growth and profits. There are global demands for U.S. goods, services, and technology that allow American firms to be successful even in a competitive environment.

Taking your company international dramatically expands the market for its goods and services. It may even extend the life cycle of current products. (Mature products have the advantage of better margins, resulting in higher profits.)

Though business cycles exist throughout the economic world, the cycles in different parts of the globe are rarely in synch. An international company can avoid the worst effects of a bad phase of the cycle in one region by increasing revenues in geographical areas that are experiencing a more favorable phase. Global rather than product diversification is thus an excellent strategy for a growing company.

BASIC ISSUES

The manager who assumes responsibility for an international project must deal with the many issues unique to the international environment. Cultural issues of language, customs, and laws are the first to come to mind, but there are many others. Some exist in only certain parts of the world, such as the fact that the weekend in the Middle East falls on Thursday and Friday rather than the more common Saturday and Sunday, which means that everyday business communications must be carefully scheduled. The Internet helps, but not all communications can be conducted via e-mail.

Race and national origin as an issue is not as common as it used to be. It remains a problem primarily in the Middle East. Some governments limit personnel working on a project in their country to nationalities and races they consider friendly.

As more women rise to management positions in American firms, the previously all-male business relationships in some regions of the global marketplace are being challenged to accept that change. Some social rules apply uniquely to women. American companies operating abroad must understand these rules to help them achieve and maintain the business relationships that are beneficial and desired by both parties.

The project manager must also be sensitive to age issues. In international business, because personal relationships precede business, it is usually wiser if the counterparts are near the same age. The relatively young senior executives of some American firms can have difficulties in developing personal relationships with customer counterparts who are 10 or 15 years senior.

The trend in the United States over the past two decades has been toward reduced formality in all matters. We dress casually, call each other by first names even on first introduction, and assume a familiarity that is often uncomfortable for people from other cultures and countries. In international business, formality should prevail in all matters—whether making an introduction, proffering a gift, offering a business card, making a dinner invitation, or corresponding on business matters. There are protocols that must be observed in all interactions. A manager who is socially inept can irreparably damage an international business relationship.

After some months, a local representative in Taiwan was able to secure an appointment with an influential general in the Army of Taiwan. The marketing manager arrived in country two days early to ensure that he was prepared for his presentation to the officer. However, for reasons never fully explained, he was one hour late for the meeting, and though he called to let the general's office know, the meeting was cancelled. Over the next four years, the local representative was not able to make another appointment with the general or anyone else in his office.

Fortunately for Americans, English has become the language of business and diplomacy throughout the world. Letters, contracts, and discussions are routinely conducted in English. English is a precise language in the sense that any thought can be expressed in well-constructed English sentences. The challenge is to keep the sentences simple and declarative, easy to translate, and to put as much care in the writing as the customer surely will in the reading.

In international business relationships, it is common to exchange gifts. In choosing gifts the project manager should seek the advice of an in-country advisor to avoid any inadvertent offense. There is a growing trend for customers to prefer gifts for their children rather than themselves, for instance, but that preference can vary with the locality.

RISKS AND DISADVANTAGES

While there are benefits to going international and unique issues to be addressed, there are also risks and possible disadvantages.

Foremost is the competitive environment, which is often hostile and stacked unfairly against American companies. The advantage the U.S. firm has is the international appeal of U.S. products and services and its ability to bring into the competition something unique and otherwise unavailable to the customer.

For larger contracts in Europe, American firms must deal with consortiums that are formed to execute particular projects. A consortium tends to exclude any outside company unless it can offer something needed by the customer that none of the consortium members can provide. This "something unique" can be a product, a service, technology, or even a significantly better price. The most direct approach for a U.S. company in this situation is to seek a position as a second or third-tier subcontractor to a consortium member.

The international project is exposed to unique legal issues. Sometimes the laws of the United States can be imposed in the contract, but most often it is governed by the laws of the host country. In these cases, to mitigate risk, it is wise to negotiate a contract clause that requires arbitration in a neutral country, such as England. Litigation and arbitration should be a last resort. Well-written contracts and statements of work will help avoid misunderstandings that can result in these unpleasant actions.

Labor issues overseas differ from those in the United States. In many countries there are protections from layoffs and discharges that can cost a company dearly if it is unaware of the governing law. For instance, Americans are accustomed to relatively short vacations and to having management approve requests for time off. Outside the United States, six-week vacations are the norm, as are six or more weeks of sick leave. During the month of August, Europe is virtually closed for business. Plants shut down to give the employees four of their six weeks of vacation. When vacations are combined with numerous national, regional, community, and religious holidays, the number of workdays annually tends to be much lower than in the United States. The international project manager must build these factors into the overseas schedule.

Another risk for the international project manager is the time-dependent relative value of currencies. Revenues in one currency and expenses in another can create a high risk for the project unless the manager takes action to reduce or eliminate fluctuations. Among the variety of methods of reducing risks are:

• Contracting in U.S. dollars.

• Seeking a large up-front payment.

• Buying forward.

• Using letters of credit.

The international company must be prepared to modify its products according to the customs, laws, and preferences of the country where the project is sited. The sales message must be modified not only in language, but also in message content. There have been some well-publicized mistakes in getting the appropriate message across.

The U.S. government requires export licenses for a large number of products. Most are issued by the Departments of Commerce and State, but other departments may exercise authority over products falling within their jurisdiction. Licenses must be in place before work on the project begins (with rare exceptions), and the licensing process can take months to complete.

Resources available to the business seeking to break into international markets run the gamut from U.S. government agencies interested in increasing exports to private firms in the business of helping companies find contacts and customers. Government agencies include:

• The Small Business Administration.

• The Department of Commerce.

• The Department of Agriculture.

Among private-sector exporters associations are World Trade Centers, the American Association of Exporters and Importers, and the Small Business Exporter Association. There are also trade associations, chambers of commerce, foreign embassies and consulates, and in-country trade representatives. All these resources can provide contacts as well as a venue in which the company can begin to build the necessary relationships on which to build future business.

The most important phase of an international project is planning. Every serious problem can be traced back to a poor plan. We Americans like to "get on with it" and make adjustments later. Though that aspect of our national personality has its admirable qualities, for an international project manager it can be ruinous. A well-thought-out plan is a must.

The Japanese tend to plan, evaluate the plan, and re-evaluate the plan before they ever get started on a project, but when they are ready, they are really ready. They have the design, the interfaces, and the functions well documented. They are so prepared for the work that they can be confident that the project will succeed.

ORGANIZING THE PROJECT

In Chapter 5, I explained how to draw up a game plan. The effort starts during the marketing phase and continues through execution and verification. The game plan—which later transforms into the Integrated Master Plan for the project—must be detailed and all-inclusive. At a minimum, it includes:

- Project description.

- Marketing plan.

- Description and analysis of the competition.

- Manager's vision of the project.

- List of key personnel.

- Financial data.

The plan is the road map for the project. It must be posted in the project room. It must be available to all team members and referred to often during the course of the project. The project's PERT chart is derived from the plan.

An international project imposes additional considerations for organizing and staffing beyond those of a domestic project. Among such factors are:

- The culture of the country.

- An incentive plan for project completion.

- An in-country office and staff.

- Employee overseas housing and transportation.

- Medical care.

- Dependent schooling.

- Inherent difficulties of control.

- Local subcontractors.

- Local labor.

Each item has associated costs that must be weighed against employee benefit and morale. Turnover of overseas personnel can result in high costs to the project in terms of both additional dollars and schedule slippage. It is therefore important that employee morale rate high on the project manager's priority list.

The key to a smooth-running project is to foresee, and then head off, problems. Unless you're a manager who enjoys rushing about with great fanfare from crisis to crisis to demonstrate how busy and effective you are, heading off problems before they become crises and mitigating risks produce a project that not only runs smoothly but also meets all its goals. Project difficulties must be addressed promptly. Otherwise, like a toothache, they just get worse. Dragons are much easier to slay while they're in the egg stage than when they're fully grown.

In the preceding chapters, I've provided the tools necessary to foresee project difficulties. These tools are:

- The integrated master schedule and the integrated master plan.

- The risk management system.

- The metrics and quality management system.

- The financial control system.

APPLYING THE TOOLS

Management tools are just that—tools. Tools and systems, as I have reiterated, are only as effective as the skills of the manager implementing them. A skillful manager will use them far more effectively than will a less skillful one. Many managers mistakenly believe that the tools enable anyone to be a good manager. It doesn't work that way any more than giving someone a hammer will make her a carpenter.

The reports resulting from each of the tools listed must be posted in the project room, along with the project network (PERT chart). The network in its entirety is not presented in the appendixes to this book due to its sheer physical size. A map of an effective network will usually covers much of the project room's wall space. The software package used to create the project schedule will also produce the network chart. The network is a visual reference to the entire project. Connectivity is easy to follow because predecessor and successor links show what tasks and milestones will be impacted by a failure of any task along the path.

The PERT chart also shows the critical path through the project, which has no slack. "No slack" means that any slip along the critical path results in at least day-for-day slip of the project at the end of the schedule. Problems along the critical path are ignored at peril to the project. As much attention as the critical path deserves and demands, the numerous tasks just waiting to jump onto the critical path merit attention, too.

Every problem sends out early warning indicators for the observant project manager. Every problem evaluation team, commonly referred to as a Red Team, I have ever seen has been able to trace critical problems back to early warning indicators that were missed or that the project manager viewed as unimportant. The project manager must remain vigilant and ready to respond promptly to such warning signs.

Some valuable indicators of emerging problems were discussed in Chapter 7—the variance analyses for cost and schedule. As valuable as these are, alone they cannot give accurate indications of what is wrong, or how bad it can get. Other indexes and trends are needed to give clues as to the root cause.

The integrated master plan and the integrated master schedule together form the road map for the project, setting milestones to be achieved by specific dates and establishing the means to arrive at final completion and evaluation of the project. Anywhere and at any time along that road that all the elements fail to mesh, there is a clear problem to be addressed. The milestones must be set so that failure to meet any one of them does not jeopardize the success of the whole project. That is why a major milestone should be preceded by a set of smaller milestones, so that the manager can foresee and avoid any difficulty in succeeding with the major event.

The risk management program forces the members of the project team to identify potential threats to the success of the project and deal with them in advance. How successful the effort will be depends on the dedication of the project manager. Throughout the life of the project the Risk Management Board continually reviews the status of the project and of any risk items and encourages consideration of new risk items. The board should meet at least weekly and the meeting must have high priority for the members. It has been my experience that after the meeting is cancelled or postponed the first time, it quickly becomes a low priority and the risk management program ceases to be effective.

The quality management system is a valuable tool for locating and identifying faults in various processes that can create problems. It provides the means to continually improve the many processes at work in the project and forces measurement of qualitative elements. While reducing errors and faults, the quality system also reduces the probability of self-inflicted problems.

The financial control system is the most effective tool for forecasting problems, though the other tools have to be used to identify the specific cause that is producing the indicators and flags of the financial control system. This system also predicts troublesome trends early, allowing the project manager to take corrective action, and it can accurately predict the productivity required at any point in the schedule to achieve project goals.

Those four tools combined with the skills of the project manager are sufficient to predict and avoid project troubles. These are also the tools used by the Red Team in determining in retrospect what went wrong and why, and why the project manager did not take corrective action in time. That team will find any indicators overlooked by the project manager.

PREPARING FOR TROUBLE

There are basically three things that go wrong on a project:

1. The costs can rise to absorb profits or create a loss.

2. The schedule can slip, increasing the costs of maintaining and continuing the project until the entire budget is consumed and the profits are gone.

3. The delivered product does not meet the customer's standards, meaning that much of the project has to be repeated. This reflects the old adage, "There's never enough time to do it right, but there's always enough time to do it over."

The result of any of these problem types is the same—no profit.

Real-world problems would be much easier to solve if they appeared one at a time, as they do in an academic study. Normally, though, there are multiple gremlins at work. The challenge is to isolate, evaluate, and miti-gate or to eliminate the cause of any variance. Eliminating the source will keep the problem from getting progressively worse, but that alone will not get the project back on track. That will take additional effort, and perhaps additional resources.

Two of the subsystems of the Europistania Log Cabin Project have the potential to cause significant difficulties when they are installed overseas for the first time. They are (1) the security system associated with the access subsystem and (2) the communication subsystem with its three sub-ordinate systems.

THE SECURITY SYSTEM

For the security system, the customer wants the design and the equipment to be of U.S. manufacture. Its primary power source will have to be what is available within Europistania, which is different from the U.S. standard. Backup power will be battery generated. The specifications will include not only all these facts but also how long the battery source will have to oper-ate in an emergency.

Further, the customer requires that this system, and the communica-tions system, be installed using only American labor. This is an unusual requirement, but in two countries where the company I was with was to install systems related to security, the customer believed he would not be able to maintain secrecy if he used his own countrymen for installing the system.

There are two potential risks associated with the security system:

1. It will require an export license because it is on the CCL of the Department of Commerce, and it may also include restrictions by the Department of State.

2. Installing it for the first time overseas would be an unacceptable risk to the project manager: Because of the concern for terrorism in Europistania, the security system is specified to contain infrared, visual, audio, and seismic alert technologies.

To mitigate these risks, the project manager decides to install and test the security system in the United States before shipping it overseas.

Further, he decides that the system should be installed in the supplier's plant but that his own team will evaluate and test the system.

Sometimes the root of a problem is well hidden, and though the financial control system shows indicators, finding the cause and eliminating it can prove difficult, if not impossible. The example that domestic suppliers can present the same risks to a project as overseas suppliers.

A few years ago, a company accepted a project to upgrade communications at a number of airports in a European country. The technical job was challenging. The radio and telephone-switching system was to be one of the most advanced in the world.

There were a few telecommunications switching companies in the United States and elsewhere, but none had produced such a sophisticated switching system or telephone instrument. The project manager requested proposals from three suppliers. One stood out as being almost 100 percent compliant with the specifications. After some analysis of all the proposals, that supplier was selected.

Much later, in the testing phase in plant, it was discovered that many of the requirements had not been met. A further review indicated that the responses to the specifications had been in some cases worded: "Fully compliant, except for. . . ." A belated careful reading of the exception revealed that the switching system was, in fact, noncompliant.

There was plenty of blame to spread around for this error, and it cost the company dearly to correct the mistake.

Could that risk have been avoided? Clearly. In this case, as the prospective systems were being reviewed, there was a transition of technical leadership on the project, so those with the most experience failed to review in detail the responses from the candidates. Upper management knew that the same switching system had been delivered to another customer, and that customer was satisfied. What management did not know, or did not understand, was that the new requirements were not the same as for the system previously delivered.

There were other warnings, too. Financial reports showed that labor was costing about what was expected but progress was slow, and in some cases nonexistent, so the schedule was in trouble. That subsystem was on the project's critical path.

As happens with most major difficulties, these problems in the example did not exist in isolation. There were numerous other problems with the subcontractor that consumed much of the project's budget and tended to diffuse exposure of the particular problem, making it difficult to discern specific discrepancies. This was an extreme case of a problem that began early but was undetected for a number of reasons until it had become a full-grown dragon.

Though the manager of the Log Cabin project decided to build and test the security system in the supplier's plant before shipping it overseas, he had not included that effort in his initial planning. The new risk mitigation action now must be incorporated into the schedule and funded. Looking at Line 114 (Appendix A), the schedule calls for 30 days of trade study on whether to buy the system overseas or domestically. The customer made that decision quickly, so the budget and schedule for that study, which is no longer required, can be diverted to this new task.

The next step the manager can take is to convince the supplier that it is in her best interest, as risk mitigation, to build and test the system within the budget she already has. There is ample evidence that solving problems stateside is much less expensive that solving them overseas, so this proposal has a good chance of being accepted. If so, the project manager has created a work-around within the existing budget while reducing an element of risk later in the project. Additionally, by testing the system in-plant, he will reduce the time needed for testing overseas, possibly creating slack in the schedule at a crucial time.

THE COMMUNICATIONS SYSTEM

The communications subsystem presents similar problems, but with additional complexities. The obvious approach is to have the telephone system made locally, given that the equipment interfaces overseas differ from those in the United States. Another option may be an American-made closed system with a custom interface to the local telephone network. The closed system would have an automatic switching system or PABX to provide the interface between the internal telephone system and the external telephone network.

There are both cost and technical issues to be resolved: Here, cost favors the American system and technology favors the overseas system. This is a good candidate for a trade study but that has not been included in the schedule or the budget. The project manager must decide whether to commit management reserve funds to the study, or perhaps to make other adjustments in the Integrated Management Plan to adjust the budget.

The entertainment system will be of local manufacture, so the plan or budget need not be adjusted for that part of the communications system.

The computer and information technology (IT) system is to be of American manufacture, but that will not require a trade study because it was part of the original proposal submitted. The only significant technical issue is again the matter of interface with the telecommunications network in country, but the technical staff have assured the project manager that it was not a significant issue.

That leaves Risk Item Number 003 (see Appendix B). Although the technical staff has assured the project manager there is not a serious problem with the interface, the company has a shortage of telecommunications engineers, who are the experts needed in the field. The project manager knows there remains some element of risk.

MATERIALS

Another concern relates to the logs for the log cabin, which raise several issues (all risk items are found in Appendix B):

- The supplier has a reputation for being late (Risk Item 001).

- The Department of Agriculture may not permit the export of the Ponderosa pine logs (not yet identified as a risk item).

- The Country of Europistania may not permit the import of foreign wood (Risk Item 004).

These types of problems are not unusual for international projects. Various blocs of countries encourage trading within the bloc and restrict imports from outside the bloc. American firms often find themselves outside the bloc and subject to import restrictions.

These are the most serious issues for the project. The contract specifies Ponderosa pines, with no option for a substitute, so any of these three issues could become a show-stopper. The project manager should have been working on them from the beginning of the proposal effort. He could not afford to wait until the contract is signed to take action.

Taking the last issue first, the in-country representative must lobby the local bureaucracy and government representatives to permit the logs to be imported. This is a good example of a situation in which enlisting the customer's assistance is appropriate. If successful, there may be strings attached to the approval, such as a maximum number or size of logs or that the logs must be treated to prevent them carrying pests into the country, and the conditions could adversely affect the project. Should that happen, there might have to be further, post-contract, negotiations with the customer.

Similarly, dealing with U.S. export restrictions means that the Department of Agriculture must be lobbied. The project manager may have to get lobbying help from the Embassy of Europistania. The point here is that there are a variety of ways to deal with government restrictions.

The time associated with obtaining the approvals from both governments restrict the options on approaching the first issue, the potentially late deliveries. The risks associated with placing orders early are too great to take, so the project manager must wait until he has approval, even if only informal, before issuing the purchase order. What he can do is to give the supplier a specification and a nonbinding intent to purchase. The supplier would then have an early indication that the order is coming and can plan accordingly.

These documents should be presented to the supplier in person by a member of the purchasing department—or the project manager himself—to lend credibility to the order. Even if the supplier will commit only to a partial delivery, so as not to increase his own risks, the project is that much better off.

The project manager finds he has scheduled only 40 percent of the price of the contract for direct offset (see Chapter 10), whereas the contract calls for 50 percent. This problem was created by the high cost of the materials being bought in the United States together with the shipping expenses compared to the cost of the labor being contracted in country.

This is an example of the project manager knowing he has a problem but underestimating its dimensions. Now, through discussions with the customer, he learns that the subcontract for labor resources does not count against the offset requirement. Only the subcontract for noble work does. At this point he realizes that he has planned for only 25 percent offset credit instead of the 40 percent he believed he had, and the 50 percent the contract calls for (Risk Item 005). He must now figure out how to make up the missing 25 percent.

The project manager has few options left. He must ask his own management to make a further investment of 25 percent of the price of the project in some related activity in country. In larger companies, there will be staff that can evaluate the need and recommend solutions to the offset problem, but in smaller companies it will fall upon management to decide how or whether to respond to the requirement. The project manager might even be chastised for misinterpreting the requirement and causing the company to commit more money to keep the project sold. This is one of the many hazards the manager of an international project must deal with.

OTHER SNARES

Sometimes even seemingly simple aspects of a project can cause cost overruns. Projects must be conducted in sequence. Something out of sequence can cause the entire project to be delayed.

> The project to improve airport communications in Europe involved assembly into equipment racks of a large number of off-the-shelf components. Although there were some technical complexities, one of the biggest problems was relatively non-technical: the cables interconnecting the off-the-shelf equipment. Design of the cables was scheduled for early in the project, but the group responsible for the design didn't start until much later. While the leader of the group was reassigned and the new leader took time to get oriented, the rest of the project was moving forward. The design of some of the cables turned out to be more difficult that expected and the total number of cables required almost tripled. Once the project manager finally realized the magnitude of the problem, he had to double the cable staff and approve extensive overtime. That made the cable effort part of the critical path, resulting in a slip at the end of the project.

Another common difficulty with international projects is staffing the overseas phase. Though there will be a few employees willing to make an early commitment to go overseas, many will delay decision as long as possible hoping for a better "package."

A project manager for a telecommunications enhancement program in Greece had difficulty finding qualified company engineers willing to live in remote parts of Greece for a whole year. His main problem was a much more attractive competing project in France. Paris was naturally more appealing to them than villages in Northern Greece.

His solution was to use temporary employees from an agency specializing in technical personnel. Though his labor costs were marginally higher than for company employees, he was able to offer a standard benefits package without having to adjust the package to the preferences of each employee. He saved enough on the benefits to cover the difference in labor rates.

Overseas staff who decide to come home before the project is finished create another problem. Sometimes the employee is dissatisfied. Often the departure is precipitated by the employee's family. It takes some time to complete the turnover cycle of sending employee and family home and finding a replacement, acquiring passports and visas, and the other administrative requirements for overseas travel. Such key-person turnover presents a significant schedule risk—one that will happen on every project.

Since it's difficult to forecast which employee might want to come home—you wouldn't send them in the first place if you knew they would place this demand on you—it's not possible to have a backup ready for everyone. Yet that's what you have to do to the extent you can: Identify the key positions or skills that require backup, get tentative commitments, and do as many of administrative measures as you can in advance for the potential replacements. None of this assures complete coverage, but it does reduce risk.

Another approach that can work if the project has efforts in-plant and in-country at the same time is to rotate personnel through the overseas phase. Any additional travel costs from rotation are more than made up by the savings in the other support costs, such as housing and overseas bonuses.

Export licenses and technical assistance agreements for the transfer of technology are prime causes of schedule delays for international projects. Not only may the Department of Commerce not issue an export license for specific items on the bill of materials that appear on the Department of Commerce's CCL but the Department of State may even restrict because they might end up with the wrong end user. This can happen with electronic equipment that could be converted to military or terrorist use. Should this occur, the design would have to be modified to use different components. If that is not possible, then the *force majeure* clause of the contract may be the only recourse. Though the CCL is of course checked in the course of preparing the proposal, it has been known to change, to the detriment of contracts just completed.

Technical assistance agreements can be more risky for two reasons:

1. The customer has to be a signatory and the end user has to be identified.

2. It can be difficult to obtain approval for any transfer of technology.

Any delay, no matter who causes it, can result in a schedule slip. Just as an added note, software that was *modified* in the United States becomes U.S. technology, even if the basic software was designed outside the country. Once software has been modified, the company may have to obtain approval of the Department of State even to return the software code to the country that originally produced it.

Many companies have sought to have a technical assistance agreement worded to include conditions the company was unable to negotiate into the basic contract. The argument presented to the customer would be that the U.S. government required that wording to obtain the license to export. Unless this is the literal truth, this is a bad approach. If it is the truth, the State Department's approval document will specify the necessary conditions. If not, the astute customer will recognize the attempt and refuse to sign the agreement. You cannot send the document to the State Department for approval until the customer has signed it and certified the end user of the technology. So, if schedule is critical, and it always is, keep the request straightforward, get the signatures, and start the process through the State Department as early as possible.

A technical assistance agreement can be initiated even during the proposal stage to ensure that it is in place when you need it. Even if the contract has not yet been awarded, with the customer's cooperation you can nevertheless initiate the request. In addition to the customer's signature on the document, you may also need a nonbinding letter of intent from him to show good faith to the State Department.

Other factors can affect the schedule. For instance, weather can play a role.

> In Portugal, a local subcontractor was engaged to dig the trenches necessary to house cables between facilities. Though the weather in Portugal is generally mild all year, the ground around Beja is frozen in the winter, and the subcontractor had no heavy trenching machines, only manpower, to do the job. The schedule had to be adjusted or the subcontractor fees significantly increased. The project manager adjusted the schedule to allow the trenching to be done after the ground thawed. Fortunately, that part of the schedule was not on the critical path.

Local safety and environmental regulations can also force design changes. Many of these are familiar only to those who enforce them and those who work with them regularly. It is the responsibility of the in-country office to find out and understand what regulations will affect the project.

A typical local rule applies to radio transmitters: Every country has a government office that approves the use of radio frequencies. Just because a certain frequency can be used for a particular purpose in the United States does not mean that it can be used for the same purpose anywhere else. Failure to gain early approval to use a desired frequency can cause cost increases and schedule delays, as well as a dissatisfied customer.

VERIFICATION

There will be a verification phase at the end of every project. This is when the project manager demonstrates that he has met the terms of all the specifications, the SOW, and the contract. The exit criteria were already decided during negotiations and are themselves part of the SOW, which usually contains or has attached a Verification Cross Reference Index (VCRI). The VCRI takes every requirement containing a *shall* statement and states how it will be verified—test, demonstration, analysis, or inspection.

Each verification method has is own set of procedures, test being the most rigorous. Testing often involves breaking something or stressing an element of the system to the extent of a specified parameter. Destruction of the item is common. Examples of destructive tests would include a missile test in which the missile is destroyed when it hits the target, or a drop test for electronic equipment. Non-destructive tests could include the verification that a radar could detect a target of a specified size, speed, and distance.

Demonstration procedures don't usually include any destruction. In fact, destruction of the item under demonstration would mean that it has failed verification (unless the item is a missile). Essentially, in a demonstration, the operator does what the user would do during normal operation and verifies that the result is what is expected. For example, depressing a "start" button actually starts the process specified.

Analysis is used when other means are not feasible. The procedures would be designed to prove that the item performs, or would perform, as required. Often the customer is involved in design of the analysis process to assure his confidence in the verification. For example, frequency interference, or a lack thereof, is often subjected to analysis.

Inspection is used for the more mundane verification. By inspection, we verify that the light is red, for example, or that electrical safety labels have been installed.

It is during this verification phase that the project is at greatest risk for customer non-acceptance by the customer. If not all the requirements are found to have been met, how many and which failures constitute failure to perform the contract as a whole? This is something that should have been agreed to before the project begins. Additionally, the contractor must be allowed a reasonable opportunity to correct the deficiency.

The two most technical aspects of the Europistania Log Cabin Project are the security and the communications subsystems. For both, the project manager required that the system be installed in-plant and verified there. The customer would be invited to observe the verification. Later, when the two subsystems were installed in country, total project verification should go well. Any problems due to the different installation circumstances would be much easier to correct than if the systems had not already been verified separately.

The customer's approval of the verification results not only terminates that portion of the project, it initiates the warranty period. In Europe, a two-year warranty period is common, but elsewhere 90 days to a year is the norm.

Time and effort spent in planning the project reap huge benefits at the end in terms of cost control, schedule maintenance, and customer satisfaction. Most problems, like those I have mentioned, can be avoided with early detailed planning.

RECAPITULATION

Managing a project is essentially following a plan and managing any problems that may arise. The key to a successful international project is to foresee and head off problems. Though this book has provided tools for managing a project to a successful conclusion, a skilled project manager is required to make them effective.

The three things that can go wrong with a project are:

1. Cost increases.
2. Schedule delays.
3. Customer dissatisfaction.

Quite often these problems come in groups, not in single file, which means that they are difficult to isolate and resolve. Still, there are always indicators for the alert project manager to observe that will permit him to take timely action. That way lies success in international projects.

APPENDIX A

GANTT CHART FOR THE EUROPISTANIA LOG CABIN PROJECT

This Gantt Chart for the Europistania Log Cabin Project has been created for illustrative purposes only. Should, by some quirk of fate, you have such a project, it is not recommended that you use the chart verbatim. The elements on the chart have been created to illustrate specific points; though realistic, they are not intended to be applied in real life.

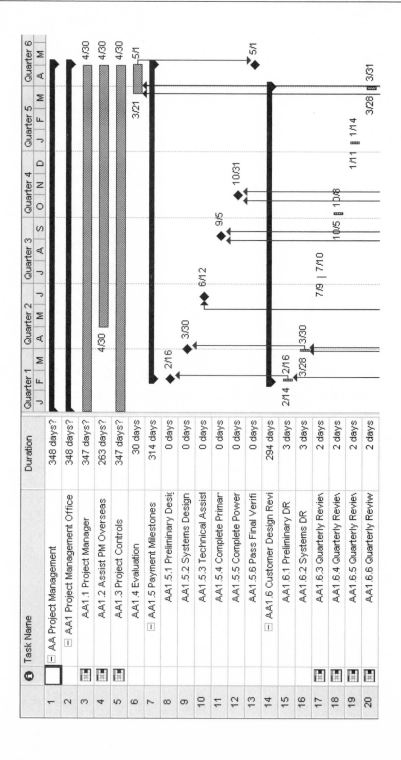

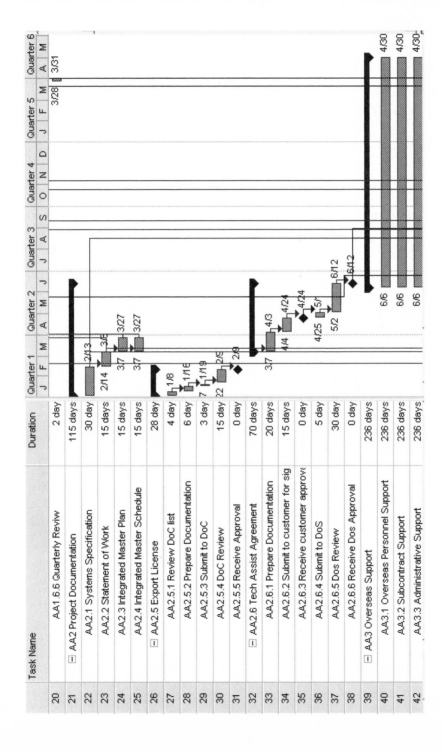

	Task Name	Duration
43	AB Land Preparation	36 days
44	AB1 Clear the Land	23 day
45	AB1.1 Contract clearing crew	10 day
46	AB1.2 Clear trees	10 day
47	AB1.3 Clear brush/grass	3 day
48	AB2 Remove debris	3 day
49	AB3 Grading of land	8 day
50	AB3.1 Stake the land	2 day
51	AB3.2 Grading	6 day
52	AB4 Trenching	2 days
53	AB4.1 Let Contract	1 day
54	AB4.2 Monitor Trenching	1 day
55	AC Primary Structure	219 days
56	AC1 Design and Architecture Drawings	30 days
57	AC2 Superstructure	101 days
58	AC2.1 Design and Specifications	30 day
59	AC2.2 Acquire materials for superstruc	47 days
60	AC2.2.1 Prepare Bill of Materials	10 day
61	AC2.2.2 Place Order for materials	5 day
62	AC2.2.3 Ship Materials	30 day
63	AC2.2.4 Transport materials to site	2 day

	Task Name	Duration
64	⊟ AC2.3 Lay Foundation	11 day
65	AC2.3.1 Let Contract	5 day
66	AC2.3.2 Monitor foundation	6 day
67	⊟ AC2.4 Construct Exterior Walls	26 day
68	AC2.4.1 Framing	11 day
69	AC2.4.2 Exterior walls	15 day
70	⊟ AC3 Roof	77 days
71	AC3.1 Design and Specifications	15 days
72	⊟ AC3.2 Acquire materials for roof	42 day
73	AC3.2.1 Prepare Bill of Materials	5 day
74	AC3.2.2 Place order for materials	5 day
75	AC3.2.3 Ship materials	30 day
76	AC3.2.4 Transport materials to site	2 day
77	⊟ AC3.3 Construct Roof	20 day
78	AC3.3.1 Framing of Roof	5 day
79	AC3.3.2 Roof Tiles	15 day

Gantt chart table:

	Task Name	Duration
80	⊟ AC4 Interior Construction	219 day
81	AC4.1 Design and Specifications	60 day
82	⊟ AC4.2 Furnishings	129 day
83	AC4.2.1 Selection of furnishings	10 day
84	AC4.2.2 Bill of Materials	30 day
85	AC4.2.3 Ship furnishings	30 day
86	AC4.2.4 Transport to site	2 day
87	AC4.2.5 Install furnishings	2 day
88	⊟ AC4.3 Wall Designs and Materials	37 day
89	AC4.3.1 Bill of Materials	30 day
90	AC4.3.2 Purchase Materials (Local)	5 day
91	AC4.3.3 Transport materials to site	2 day
92	⊟ AC4.4 Construct Interior	65 day
93	AC4.4.1 Install interior walls	30 day
94	AC4.4.2 Interior Finishing	30 day
95	AC4.4.3 Interior Painting	5 day

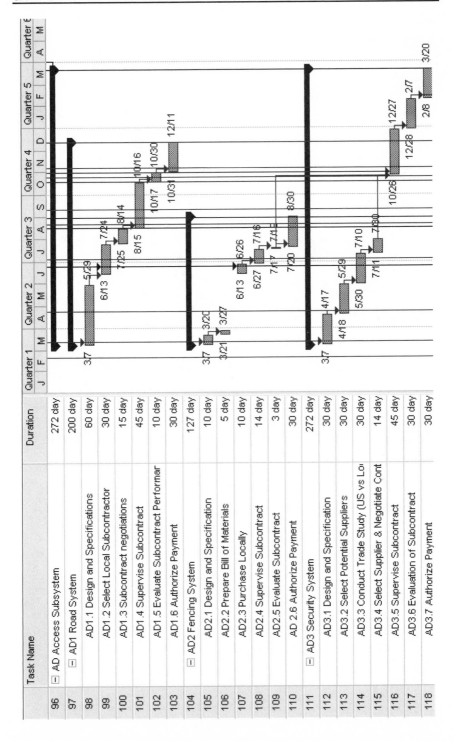

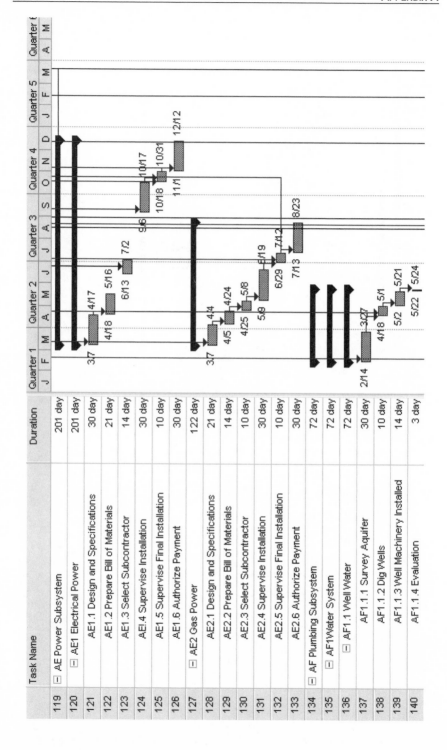

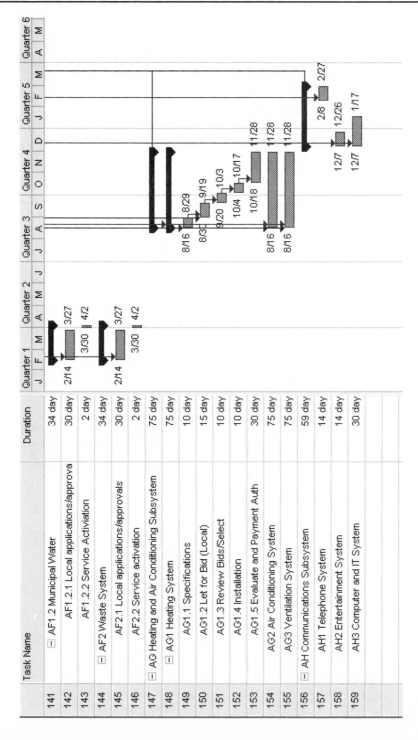

APPENDIX B

RISK MANAGEMENT FORMS FOR THE EUROPISTANIA LOG CABIN PROJECT

The risks identified in these sample forms for the Risk Management Program may or may not be realistic, either in subject or evaluation; they are for illustration only.

Black ink on the form entries indicates an initial entry to the form. Such an entry would be made by the person identifying the risk item for review. Items in italic are actions and modifications directed by the Risk Management Board. For illustration purposes, some original entries have been retained and the italic entries shown alongside.

PROJECT RISK LOG

No.	Level	Title	I/E	Definition	Assigned to	Submitted	Will Occur	To Close	Closed
001	Med	Late Delivery of Logs	E	The sole supplier of Ponderosa Pines has a reputation for lateness	Karen S.	1/3/XX	6/20/XX	5/30/XX	
002	High	Tech Assist Agreement	E	The schedule includes only 60 working days for State Department approval. It sometimes takes up to six months.	Ralph P.	1/3/XX	6/10/XX	5/2/XX	
003	Med	Telecom Engrs	I	The critical shortage of telecom engineers in the company will impact a major subsystem.	Keith S.	1/3/XX	12/9/XX	11/1/XX	
004	High	Import of Logs	E	In-Country rep notified project manager that Europistania may limit or prohibit the import of complete logs from outside the country, due to their own wood export industry.	Mike G.	1/3/XX	4/22/XX	4/4/XX	
005	Med	Offset Require-ment	I/E	Contract requires a fifty percent offset in a related business activity. This will require company funding outside the project.	Janet T.	1/3/XX	4/1/XX	3/4/XX	
006	Low	Overseas Staff	I	Lack of commitment for the overseas staff places the schedule at risk.	Bruce C.	1/3/XX	6/6/XX	4/15/XX	
007	Med	Staff Inexperience	I	No one on the staff has any experience in specifying or installing entertainment systems overseas.	Todd S.	1/3/XX	12/9/XX	3/15/XX	
008	Low	Quality Assurance	I	Recently approved standard processes have not been verified.	Cathy B.	1/3/XX			

RISK IDENTIFICIATION AND STATUS—LATE DELIVERY OF LOGS

Risk Level: **Med**

Risk Number: **001**   Originator: **F. Pasquel**   Risk Assigned to: **Karen S.**

Date Submitted	Date Reviewed	Date Risk Will Occur	Date Risk to Close	Date Close	Internal or External Risk?	Last Update
1/3/XX	1/5/XX	6/20/XX	5/30XX			1/5/XX

Definition of the Risk and the Baseline Document

There is only one supplier of Ponderosa Pine logs in the United States and he has a reputation for late deliveries. The shortest delivery time on an order this size has been over 2 months. This will impact both the Contract and the Statement of Work, and may have an impact on the System Specification.

Probability of Occurrence (Pf): **0.5**

Consequence of Occurrence (Cf): **0.9 0.8**

Risk Factor (Rf): **4.5 4.0**

Cost Level Cf: **5**

Discussion of Cost Impact: The cost of a 60 day delay with 30 people on the project would be as much as $360,000

Schedule Level Cf: **9 8**

Discussion of Schedule Impact: **Most likely the delay would be about 40 days.**

Technical Level Cf: **0**

Discussion of Technical Impact: None noted

Operational Level Cf: **0**

Discussion of Operational Impact: None noted

		Determination of Cf			Determination of Rf
Cost	**Schedule**	**Technical**	**Operational**	**Level**	Rf = Cf X Pf
< 1 % of TC	< 10 days	low perf, minor chgs	Degraded	Low (1-3)	High, Rf > 5.5
< 5% of TC	< 30 days	low perf, mod chgs	System Threat	Med (4-6)	Med, 5.5>Rf>2.5
> 5% of TC	> 30 days	Unaccep perf, maj chgs	System Failure	High (7-9)	Low, Rf < 2.5

ACTION PLAN STATUS - LATE DELIVERY OF LOGS

Risk Number **001**   Risk Level **Medium**   Last Update **1/30/XX**

No.	ACTION PLAN	STATUS	COMMENTS
1	Contact supplier to determine estimated time from order to delivery. Consider placing order early, if Risk Item #004 is eliminated.	Contact attempted, but responsible person is out of town. 1/15/XX	**ASSIGNEE Karen S.** DUE DATE **1/20/XX**
2	Break the delivery into two phases, with ½ delivered on schedule and the second half delivered 30 days late.		ASSIGNEE **Karen S.** DUE DATE **2/15/XX**
3	Consider an incentive payment for early delivery,		ASSIGNEE **Karen S.** DUE DATE **3/30/XX**
			ASSIGNEE DUE DATE

FORMULAS WITH THE RISK MANAGEMENT PROGRAM

Consequence of Occurrence

Element	Criterion	Factor (Cf)
Cost	Consequence is less than 1% of total cost.	Low (1-3)
	Consequence is less than 5% of total cost.	Med (4-6)
	Consequence is more than 5% of total cost.	High (7-9)
Schedule	Consequence is less than 10 days.	Low (1-3)
	Consequence is less than 30 days.	Med (4-6)
	Consequence is more than 30 days.	High (7-9)
Technical	Low performance, requires minor changes.	Low (1-3)
	Low performance, requires moderate changes.	Med (4-6)
	Unacceptable performance, requires major changes.	High (7-9)
Operational	Degraded operations. Low (1-3)	
	System threat. Med (4-6)	
	System failure. High (7-9)	

Risk factor (Rf) =

Probability of occurrence (Pf) x Consequence of occurrance (Cf) [ranges from 1 to 9].

$Rf = Pf \times Cf$.

$Rf > 5.5$ represents a high risk.

$Rf\ 5.5 > Rf > 2.5$ represents a medium risk.

$Rf < 2.5$ represents a low risk.

APPENDIX C
WORK BREAKDOWN
STRUCTURE

This appendix shows the Work Breakdown Structure (WBS) in its entirety. It may in some cases require further breakdown into tasks of shorter duration, but that would normally be left to the CAM managers. The project manager rarely has sufficient in-depth knowledge of all the elements of the project to complete the WBS to that level.

WORK BREAKDOWN STRUCTURE FOR THE EUROPISTANIA LOG CABIN

A Log Cabin System
  AA Project Management
    AA1 Project Management Office (PMO)
      AA1.1 Project Manager
      AA1.2 Assist PM (Overseas)
      AA1.3 Project Controls
    AA2 Project Documentation
      AA2.1 Systems Specification
      AA2.2 Statement of Work
      AA2.3 Integrated Master Plan
      AA2.4 Integrated Master Schedule
      AA2.5 Export Licenses
        AA2.5.1 Review DoC List
        AA2.5.2 Prepare Documentation
        AA2.5.3 Submit to Dept of Commerce
      AA2.6 Technical Assistance Agreement
        AA2.6.1 Prepare Documentation
        AA2.6.2 Submit for Customer's approval
        AA2.6.3 Submit to US Dept of State
    AA3 Overseas Support
  AB Land Preparation
    AB1 Clearing
    AB2 Remove Debris
    AB3 Grading
    AB4 Trenching
  AC Primary Structure Subsystem
    AC1 Design and Architectural Drawings
    AC2 Superstructure
      AC2.1 Design
      AC2.2 Acquire materials for primary structure
      AC2.3 Ship materials
      AC2.4 Transport materials to site
      AC2.5 Lay foundation
      AC2.6 Construct superstructure
    AC3 Roof
      AC3.1 Design
      AC3.2 Acquire materials for roof (local purchase)
      AC3.3 Transport materials to site
      AC3.4 Construct roof
    AC4 Interior
      AC4.1 Design
      AC4.2 Acquire materials and furniture
      AC4.3 Ship materials
      AC4.4 Transport materials to site
      AC4.5 Construct interior
      AC4.6 Install furnishings

WORK BREAKDOWN STRUCTURE FOR THE EUROPISTANIA LOG CABIN, CONT'D

AD Access Subsystem
- AD 1 Road System
  - AD1.1 Design and specifications
  - AD1.1.1 Road base
  - AD1.1.2 Road surface
  - AD1.2 Select local subcontractor
  - AD1.3 Negotiate subcontract
  - AD1.4 Supervision of subcontractor
  - AD1.5 Evaluation of subcontractor performance
  - AD1.6 Authorization for payment to subcontractor
- AD2 Fencing System
  - AD2.1 Design
  - AD2.2 Acquire materials locally
  - AD2.3 Construct fence
- AD3 Security System
  - AD3.1 Design and specification
  - AD3.2 List potential suppliers
  - AD3.3 Tradeoff study (local versus U.S. supplier)
  - AD3.4 Select supplier
  - AD3.5 Negotiate subcontract
  - AD3.6 Supervision of subcontractor
  - AD3.7 Evaluation of subcontractor performance
  - AD3.8 Authorization for payment to subcontractor

AE Power Subsystem
- AE1 Electrical power
- AE2 Gas power

AF Plumbing Subsystem
- AF1 Water system
  - AF1.1 Well water
  - AF1.2 Municipal water
- AF2 Waste Subsystem

AG Heating and Air Conditioning Subsystem
- AG1 Heating system
- AG2 Air Conditioning system
- AG3 Ventilation system (Item reserved if needed)

AH Communications Subsystem
- AH1 Telephone system
- AH2 Entertainment system
- AH3 Computer and Internet system

APPENDIX D
GLOSSARY OF ACRONYMS

ACWP . . . . Actual Cost of Work Performed
BAG . . . . Budget at Completion
BB . . . . Black Belt
BCWP . . . . Budgeted Cost of Work Performed
BOWS . . . . Budgeted Cost of Work Scheduled
BXA . . . . Department of Commerce Bureau of Export Controls
CAM . . . . Cost Account Manager
CBB . . . . Contract Budget Baseline
CCL . . . . Commercial Control List
Cf . . . . Consequence of Occurrence (of a risk item)
CPI . . . . Cost Performance Index
CPIF . . . . Cost-Plus-Incentive-Fee
CV . . . . Cost Variance
DEC . . . . District Export Council
EAC . . . . Estimate at Completion
EAR . . . . Export Administration Regulations
EPCI . . . . Enhanced Proliferation Control Initiative
FFP . . . . Firm Fixed Price
EMS . . . . Foreign Military Sales
FPI . . . . Fixed-Price Incentive
GB . . . . Green Belt
IFB . . . . Information for Bidders

IMP . . . . Integrated Master Plan
IMS . . . . Integrated Master Schedule
INCOTERMS . . . . . International Commercial TERMS
IPT . . . . Integrated Product Team
ISO . . . . International Standards Organization
IT . . . . Information Technology
ITA . . . . International Trade Administration
LOE . . . . Level of Effort
LRE . . . . Latest Revised Estimate
MBB . . . . Master Black Belt
MR . . . . Management Reserve
ODC . . . . Other Direct Charges
PABX . . . . Private Automatic Base Exchange
PERT . . . . Program Evaluation and Review Technique
Pf . . . . Probability of Occurrence (of a risk item)
PMO . . . . Project Management Office
Rf . . . . Risk Factor
RFP . . . . Request for Proposal
RM . . . . Risk Management
RMB . . . . Risk Management Board
ROI . . . . Return on Investment
RONA . . . . Return on Net Assets
SBA . . . . Small Business Administration
SBDC . . . . Small Business Development Centers
SBI . . . . Small Business Institute
SCORE . . . . Service Corps of Retired Executives
SOW . . . . Statement of Work
SPI . . . . Schedule Performance Index
SV . . . . Schedule Variance
SWOT . . . . Strengths, Weaknesses, Opportunities, and Threats
TCPI . . . . To-Complete Performance Index
UAE . . . . United Arab Emirates
US&FCS . . . . United States and Foreign Commercial Service
USDA . . . . United States Department of Agriculture
VCRI . . . . Verification Cross Reference Index
VOC . . . . Voice of the Customer
WBS . . . . Work Breakdown Structure
WIP . . . . Work in Process
WPPS . . . . Work Package Planning Sheet

INDEX

A

Acronyms, 211-212
Action plans, 125
    Action plan status, 126
    See also Defining the project;
        Mitigation process; Risk
        management.
Actual cost of work performed
    (ACWP), 98, 99
ACWP. *See* Actual cost of work
    performed.
Age matters, 21
    See also Context of international
        projects; Cultural issues; Getting
        started.
American Association of Exporters, 47
Analysis of the competition, 56-59
    See also Game plan; Getting started.
Applying financial controls, 98-105
    Formulas, 102
    Relationship of budget allocations,
        100
    Typical financial control terms, 98
    Visual reference for terminology, 99
    See also Defining the project;
        Financial controls as a
        management tool.
Applying the tools, 179-181
    See also Executing the project
        in-country; Working the project,
        working the problems.
At-completion variance, 102

B

BAC. *See* Budget at completion.
Basic issues, 174-175
    See also Executing the project
        in-country; Working the project,
        working the problems.
Basic toolbox, 138-145

Brainstorming, 139
    Data-gathering tools, 143
    Fishbone cause and effect diagram,
        142
    Flowchart, 141
    SIPOC Diagram, 140
    Structure tree, 140
    Structure tree or tree diagram, 139
    See also Defining the project;
        Metrics and quality management.
Basics of Six Sigma, 132-135
    Defined roles, 134
    Goals, 133
    Themes, 134
    See also Defining the project;
        Metrics and quality management.
BB. *See* Black belt.
BCWP. *See* Budgeted cost of work
    performed.
BCWS. *See* Budgeted cost of work
    scheduled.
Black belt (BB), 134, 135
Boeing, 57
Brainstorming, 139
    See also Basic toolbox; Defining the
        project; Metrics and quality
        management.
Budget at completion (BAC), 98, 99
Budgeted cost of work performed
    (BCWP), 98, 99
Budgeted cost of work scheduled
    (BCWS), 98, 99
Bureau of Alcohol, Tobacco, and
    Firearms, 38
Burn rate, 62
Business and culture, 25
    See also Context of international
        projects; Getting started.
Business competition, 27-28
    See Difficulties and risks of interna-
        tional projects; Getting started.
Business/social events and women, 17